THE ESSENCE AND VALUE OF LIFE

SUNDAY ADELAJA

Sunday Adelaja
THE ESSENCE AND VALUE OF LIFE
©2018 Sunday Adelaja
ISBN 978-1983545535

Cover design by Alexander Bondaruk
Interior design by Olena Kotelnykova

TABLE OF CONTENTS

INTRODUCTION 7

PART 1
UNDERSTANDING THE VALUE OF LIFE........ 9
CHAPTER 1: WHAT REALLY IS LIFE? 11
    What Life isn't..16
    Value What you Possess 19
    The True Measure of Life 23
    Life is a Gift of Trust 26
    The Origin and Source of Life 29
CHAPTER 2: UNDERSTANDING THE
PURPOSE OF LIFE 31
    The Cost of Ignorance..............................33
    Discovering Your Purpose in Life...................37
    The Meaning of Life 39
    The True Essence of Life........................... 43
CHAPTER 3: DEADLY DISTRACTIONS
OF LIFE.. 49
    The Truth Behind Distraction 51
    Three Deadly Traps 53
    Dangers Behind these Allurements 55
    Get Free from Them................................ 58
CHAPTER 4: LIFE IS MORE THAN THIS....... 65
    The Superiority of Life 67
    What Makes or Mars Life 70
    Worry: a Distraction of Purpose...............74
    Making Profits in the Business of Life.................78

CHAPTER 5: THE VALUABLE DEVOTION OF LIFE..................................83

Two Cardinal Perspectives of Life 88

Your Set Time has Come.................................91

The Most Valuable Devotion of Life 96

The Missing Day Found 98

PART 2

HOW TO TRULY LIVE.............................. 105

CHAPTER 6: LIVING FROM GOD'S PERSPECTIVE 107

Living to Learn 109

Living by His Trademarks............................112

Living Without Regrets 116

Living with Passion and Zeal........................... 123

CHAPTER 7: LIVING FOR KINDNESS 129

The Superlative Value of Kindness.....................133

Breakthroughs of Lovingkindness.....................135

A Story of Lovingkindness............................ 136

CHAPTER 8: LIVING FOR JUSTICE 143

He Lived and Died for Justice 143

The Theory of Justice................................149

Justice: Truth in Action 150

Compassion is no Substitute for Justice 152

Be Devoted to a Life of Justice 156

Justice: a Credible Cause of Boasting.................157

Let Justice Reign 162

CHAPTER 9: LIVING FOR RIGHTEOUSNESS 165

What is Righteousness?.............................169

Favor His Righteous Cause........................172

Enduring Effects of Righteousness....................177

Organized Righteousness..180
CHAPTER 10: THE TRUE ESSENCE AND
VALUE OF LIFE 187
What Will you Devote Your Life to? 189
Live a Paradisiacal Life Everyday........................194
Your Focus Matters...196
The Glorious Essence of Life................................197
CONCLUSION...201

INTRODUCTION

For so many around the world, the subject of life has been a mystery to be unravelled. Unanswered questions and myths have pervaded their minds and lingered on persistently through the years, to the extent that life has become an unsavoury experience of unfulfilled wishes.

Even our belief systems and religious inclinations have neither satisfied nor succoured the desperate quests we have to know the truth and live life in its fullest.

I strongly believe that ignorance of life's purpose has been the bane of the colossal scale of man's atrocities, his suffering and abuse of his purpose.

Especially here, in our African continent, where there is so much religion, but too little transformation of human lives and the society at large. We are yet to comprehend and reflect a true value of the human life.

America itself isn't exclusive on this. Record shows that since 2013, there has been at least 190 school shootings in America - an average of nearly one per week. A report by the Urban Institute showed in the single school district of Washington, DC, there were at least 336 gunshots in the vicinity of schools over a single school year.

Besides, there are other forms of self-inflicted predicaments and issues prevalent in various nations of the world. These evil trends all point to the awful and unavoidable dangers that result when we are ignorant of the true essence and value of life. When we lack insight and in-depth understanding of how we ought to live, abuse is inevitable.

Ralph Waldo Emerson rightly said:

"THE PURPOSE OF LIFE IS NOT TO BE HAPPY. IT IS TO BE USEFUL, TO BE HONOURABLE, TO BE COMPASSIONATE, AND TO HAVE IT MAKE SOME DIFFERENCE THAT YOU HAVE LIVED AND LIVED WELL."

RALPH WALDO EMERSON

Moreover, the Bible says:

"If the foundations be destroyed, what can the righteous do?"

Psalms 11:3

Something is fundamentally wrong with our understanding of the concept of life. Life is not an experiment to be tried, but a journey of real purpose.

In this Book, I have attempted to provide answers based on the Eternal Source and Foundation of Life; the Author of Life Himself, God Almighty. These answers are tested and proven over time and are sure to help you live a meaningful, purposeful and honourable life.

Here you will discover the purpose of your life, how to truly live and accomplish your goals; and how your journey on earth could become an invaluable experience of boundless joy and a paradise of fulfilments.

I'm confident this singular piece will complete your missing puzzle on the pressing issues of life and bring answers to the question of what really life is and your purpose on earth.

SUNDAY ADELAJA
FOR THE LOVE OF GOD, CHURCH AND NATION

PART 1

UNDERSTANDING THE VALUE OF LIFE

CHAPTER 1

WHAT REALLY IS LIFE?

"EACH OF US HAS MEANING AND WE BRING
IT TO LIFE. IT IS A WASTE TO BE ASKING THE
QUESTION WHEN YOU ARE THE ANSWER."

JOSEPH CAMPBELL

A University graduate once told me that life is moving around in circles, how empty a definition? What do you define life to be? A puzzle? Just staying alive? Many have said that life is a mystery, but it takes the true understanding of the principles of life to live out its essence and value. Many people search far for answers that are with them, some people even go to distant planets to search for answers to life. Remember, it is a waste to be asking the question when you are the answer. These truths are what I'm about to share with you, and they have been the building blocks and guiding light in the purpose-driven kingdom life I've endeavoured to live from the very moment I encountered the Author of Life and followed His principles that govern life.

Before then, life had little or no significance to me, as an orphaned raised by my grandmother in the tropical village of Idomila, Ogun state, Western Nigeria, where we lived in a hut. In fact, during my early childhood I was of the opinion that life isn't fair and there is no God at all, because of the inexplicable difficulties that surrounded my upbringing and tragic loss of my forbears.

I was a stranger to the good things of life and was fast learning to cope with hardship as the norm. At the age of nine, I was already used to hawking around the village neighborhood on barefoot, early in the morning, selling locally made corn porridge (pap) or firewood, in order to overcome the obvious perils of hunger and provide sustenance for grandma and myself. This was how we made ends meet. This was the life I knew - a struggle for survival.

After my morning sales, I had to trek some two and a half kilometers to and from the neighboring village to attend the nearest school, and I did this on barefoot for six years.

So, I can fully identify with those who are of the opinion that life isn't fair. I do know for certain that there are many whose journey began this way or even worse, especially those from the Sub-Saharan African continent, but this is never how our story should end.

My story is different now!

My success in life is a valid proof of God's faithfulness that's available to everyone who is willing to harness the power of choice and rightly apply the principles that govern life, because every person has a right to succeed in life. Success in life is your birth-right. You were born to succeed.

You don't have to live another day in defeat, deceit or disgrace. You don't have to be a long-term victim when you were born to be an all-time victor. You can change your story and soar high in life. You have a tremendous potential for greatness; an unfathomable ability to make all-round progress. But that begins when you embrace

WHAT REALLY IS LIFE?

the timeless and ageless truths about life which I'm here to share with you.

Truth is ageless; truth is timeless. Truth cannot be modernized neither does it change with civilization. Truth remains the same from generation to generation; and it works for any person who applies it. It's no respecter of race, religion, gender or nationality. Understanding the truth about life is absolutely essential if you must live out your real essence and value. When you understand the truth, your whole journey of life becomes purpose-driven. There are many who live as wanderers on earth: having no clear-cut direction or destination, with no sense of purpose or vision; thus, making terrible blunders and hurting those around them.

Life without purpose is meaningless. Life without understanding would always culminate in failure, as many fall prey to the various traps on the pathways. You need to be well informed and prepared to truly live.

Unfortunately, there are no courses in our Schools or Higher Institutions on the subject of life. All through our years in college, no one really told us how to live; no teacher took on that course, and that's because they don't have the complete answers. As a matter of fact, nobody gets a chance to even rehearse before coming to life. There's no such thing as "life-rehearsals" as they do in movies, before showing up on the scene, life just happens, and here we are, learning along the way. And those who refuse to learn along the way; will surely lose all the way. Therefore, we must be serious about understanding the real value of life and learning the true essence of our existence so as not to end up in shameful regrets. Life is an opportunity that comes only once. You can't live twice, just once. Therefore you need to make the most of every opportunity that comes your way in life. This calls for the need of preparation; getting yourself ready to live your best every day and making the most of every opportunity.

"I WILL PREPARE AND SOME DAY MY CHANCE WILL COME"

ABRAHAM LINCOLN

Most opportunities come only once and those who are best prepared are the ones who can seize them and make the most of them. Life is a golden and amazing opportunity. Make the best of it!

Ignorance is no longer an excuse for failure in life. Quite unfortunately so many in our society are still strangers to the truths about life and as a result have continued to make blunders of their existence. It's high time we lived out the true essence of our being and exterminate the contagious ignorance prevalent in our society about life.

Ignorance is too expensive to afford. Some say what you don't know can't harm you. How untrue this is. You not knowing about the law of gravity doesn't make you get suspended in the air when you jump up. You will definitely fall down. So, what you don't know can really hurt you, and I totally agree. Friends, go for knowledge. Use all you have to get knowledge. It is the principal thing.

One of the surest dangers of ignorance is fear. Ignorance breeds fear. Ignorance about the essence and value of life breeds numerous fears. It could be fear of the unknown, fear of the future, fear of failure, all kinds of fears. This is one of the reasons many commit suicide and destroy other innocent lives, because they are ignorant of the true value of life. In our country, Nigeria, many not knowing the reason for their being kill others because they want a particular office or post. This is absolute selfishness and it's all as a result of man's ignorance of life. They don't know that life is worth more than an office. When you truly know the value of life, you will value other people's lives.

Besides, abuse of life is also a result of ignorance. My dear friend, Dr Myles Munroe, of blessed memory loved to simply define 'abuse' as 'ab-normal use,' where the purpose of something is not known, then it could be wrongly utilized.

This is a key reason behind the destructive tendencies and abusive lifestyles that are banal in our societies today, because where purpose is unknown, abuse is inevitable.

The quest to comprehend the true definition of life has also been a subject as old as human existence on earth. From the pristine days of the first created man, to our modern scientific age of over 7.5 Billion people on this planet, most that has been said or heard from philosophers, scientists and various schools of thought have been nothing more than hypothetical theories and personal concepts derived from their own experiences. We know quite well that no person builds a meaningful life on complex theories or ideologies void of substantial proofs. Even our encyclopedias stagger for words in defining the concept of life. It takes the author of a book to explain its content. Thus, it takes the Author of life to define the essence and value of life.

One remarkable characteristic of truth is simplicity. Real truths are always simple to understand. Profound truths are usually the simplest to comprehend. And when it comes to this all important subject of the meaning of life, I have found out the same is applicable, that life is simplified through the understanding and application of the laws that govern it.

WHAT LIFE ISN'T

Let not the wise boast of their wisdom or the strong boast of their strength or the rich boast of their riches, but let the one who boasts boast about this: that they have the understanding to know me, that I am the Lord, who exercises kindness, justice and righteousness on earth, for in these I delight, declares the Lord.

Jeremiah 9:23-24

In order to have a good understanding of the value of life, it's highly essential to state what life isn't. Life is of greater value than the material things we esteem. Life is more than the wisdom we pursue; more than the power we crave for; more than all the wealth and riches money can buy:

God in His eternal wisdom identified three major areas, where men wrongfully devote their lives. These three things however, are not ordinary. They are a force. In fact, they are such a compelling force that only few can withstand or resist their enticement. The Big three are: Wisdom, Power and Wealth. And He expressly informs us that the value and essence of life exceeds these. Life is of greater value than wisdom, power and wealth. Otherwise said, life isn't all about wisdom; life isn't all about power; neither is it all about riches.

This reminds me of the story of Alexander the Great, who conquered the whole world in his time and died at the age of 32. History records that after conquering so many kingdoms and was returning home, he suddenly fell ill and it took him to his death bed. With death staring him in the face, Alexander realized how his conquests, his great army, his sharp sword and all his wealth, wisdom and power were of no consequence or value anymore. His great wisdom, mighty strength, power and staggering wealth which he worked terribly hard to acquire lost their essence in the face of death.

He now longed to reach home to see his mother's face and bid her his last adieu. But, he had to accept the fact that his sinking health would not permit him to reach his distant homeland. So, the mighty conqueror lay prostrate and pale, helplessly waiting to breathe his last. He called his generals and said, *"I will depart from this world soon, I have three wishes, please carry them out without fail."* With tears flowing down their cheeks, the generals agreed to abide by their king's last wishes.

"My first desire is that," said Alexander, "My physicians must carry my coffin." After a pause, he continued, Secondly, I desire that when my coffin is being carried to the grave, the path leading to the graveyard be strewn with gold, silver and precious stones which I have collected in my treasury.

The king felt exhausted after saying this. He took a minute's rest and continued. "My third and last wish is that both my hands be kept dangling out of my coffin." The people who had gathered there wondered at the king's strange wishes. But no one dare bring the question to their lips.

Alexander's favorite general kissed his hand and pressed them to his heart. "O King, we assure you that your wishes will all be fulfilled. But tell us why do you make such strange wishes?"

At this Alexander took a deep breath and said: "I would like the world to know of three lessons I have learnt. I want my physicians to carry my coffin because people should realize that no doctor can really cure anybody. They are powerless and cannot save a person from the clutches of death. So let not people take life for granted.

The second wish of strewing gold, silver and other riches on the way to the graveyard is to tell people that not even a fraction of gold will come with me. I spent all my life earning riches but cannot take anything with me. Let people realize that it is a sheer waste of time to chase wealth.

And about my third wish of having my hands dangling out of the coffin, I wish people to know that I came empty handed into this world and empty handed I go out of this world."

Then finally he said: "Bury my body, do not build a monument, and keep my hands outside so that the world knows that the person who won the world had nothing in his hands when dying."

With these last words the King closed his eyes. Soon he let death conquer him and took his last breath.

As interesting as this story may sound, many still question its authenticity, but the message remains a vital truth that re-echoes with our subject in focus. I may not be able tell how true this enthralling story of history is, but we all can't deny the soundness of truth and understanding it portrays on how life must be lived.

Life isn't all about wisdom, power and riches. Though this is what many are pursuing today. The more these things are pursued, the more the dissatisfaction man has in life. Someone once said, all I want in life is to be a commissioner, good enough he became that. After some years, he screamed, all I want is to be a senator, he became that too. Then, he desired more. I want to be the president he said. When life is not lived for the right purpose, man craves more for wisdom, power and riches which never satisfy and could be abused. But I will show you in reality, these three are the greatest distractions there is, to understanding the value and essence of life.

VALUE WHAT YOU POSSESS

"THE ULTIMATE VALUE OF LIFE DEPENDS UPON AWARENESS AND THE POWER OF CONTEMPLATION RATHER THAN UPON MERE SURVIVAL."

ARISTOTLE

One of the most painful realizations in life is to all of a sudden discover that you had possessed things all along that you were busy looking for somewhere else. It is almost an unbearable pain to suddenly recognize the value of what you had been ignorant of, which had been in your possession. To possess something and not know its value is torturous. To own something and not be aware of it could not only be annoying, but fatal too.

Life is undoubtedly the most valuable and precious of all our earthly possessions. There is simply nothing of comparable value to life. When life is lost, all is lost. When all is lost but life, really nothing is lost. Life is head and shoulders above other things we regard as precious in this world. Tragically though, it is that same life that is often least treasured or valued by men who possess it. All men have life, but only few know its value.

To have something doesn't automatically translate to having accurate understanding of it. Most people who possess life in reality do not quite understand what they possess. That is a fundamental tragedy of life. Those who possess it are often unaware of its value.

Life is a gift, a precious gift from God and you should place great value on it. When you value something, you make worthy investments in it. Investing in yourself is one of the ways of showing the value you place on the gift of life. There are many folks who don't value what they possess. It's easy to tell from the way they treat the people around them or even the inanimate properties they possess. Your value of life is mostly reflected in your value for people, especially those around you. When you value life, you'd treat people with love and respect. Those who value life place the highest premium on their relationship with God - the Source of life. It's so pertinent that you value life. Life is a sacred gift of trust; it is your most prized possession. Once it's lost, it can't be restored. Thus, the value you place on it will determine the way you live every minute and the impact you would make during your lifetime.

One of the greatest lessons I learnt in my journey on earth is that life is not all about pleasure; it's about making positive impacts. Life is superior to all forms of pleasures that could be desired on earth. Giving yourself over to pleasure at the expense of your purpose is exchanging your soul for destruction. Life is not to be used to satisfy the traps of pleasure. Life is to be lived with values such as: honesty, kindness, justice and righteousness with a sense of vision and purpose. Life is to be lived with a passion to make positive impacts. In fact, life without a vision is meaningless. Living with vision ensures impactful living.

There is no true satisfaction in life without fulfillment of purpose. A fellow who dropped out from a University in Nigeria said he wanted to get a doctorate degree in life all so he could prove to his lecturers that he isn't a dull student. The question is, after you get the doctorate degree, what next? What will you live for? Life isn't meant to be lived to get wealth, qualifications, positions and the likes all so that people can know what you have got. The University drop out thought life is all about degrees, he didn't yet realize his reason for being. He wanted to live his life, go to school, pass exams all to come back and show some old professors that he could also do it. There would be no fulfillment in doing that. You should live your life to fulfill purpose and vision.

Not every living person is making positive impacts, because not everyone understands the value of their lives. Life is of greater value than wealth and all other forms of possessions. Life is superior to money, and neither should it be used for immoral purposes. The worth of your life is not to be compared to lands, houses, cars, clothes and the mundane things many pursue after or accumulate for selfish purposes. Your value exceeds material possessions. That is the reason, Jesus the Prince of life said:

"Take heed and beware of covetousness, for one's life does not consist in the abundance of the things he possesses."

Luke 12:15

Your life does not consist in the abundance of things you possess. Life is not defined or measured by what you have, even if you have a lot.

This brings to mind the story of a certain school mate during my years of study in the University at Belarus. He was a Nigerian student, thus we were both foreigners studying in the same institution. Being a Christian, we used to attend the same fellowship, endeavouring to keep ourselves undefiled and on zeal for the Lord in the atheistic society where we lived in. Along the line, this friend gradually began to withdraw himself from the fellowship, making excuses here and there because of his new found love: a Belarusian girl-friend. It seemed like a new exciting life for him, as he started engaging himself in all manner of things he never did prior to this time like drinking, smoking, partying from one night club to another and getting drunk. All our attempts to dissuade him from this prodigious lifestyle and unbecoming way of living fell on deaf ears. He refused all our counsels and prayers, because he was head over heels in love with this new girl. Then suddenly, his academic performance got on the decline. The University authorities started issuing complaints about his poor attitude to his studies, and not long after he earned an expulsion from the institution. To cap it all, my friend ended up an alcoholic and drug addict, wandering the streets of the strange land he came to study and died not many years afterwards of liver cirrhosis. What a sad story of life that was!

I felt terribly sad about his story and how I wish he listened and exercised some form of restraint, maybe he wouldn't have ended up in life this way. One attractive distraction led to another, and then to a calamitous end. Today, there are still so many young folks on the same highway to destruction, making this same mistake, ignoring the beckoning of others to retrace their steps and follow the way of life; to look away from the temporary pleasures of death and exercise self-restraint in order to live a meaningful life. Maybe if I had followed the same route this friend of mine chose, I wouldn't be where God has brought me today. I wouldn't have the wonderful wife and lovely children I greatly treasure; I wouldn't have been able to influence the millions of lives I did. Thank God for helping me follow the path of life, and not pursue the vain things that can't be compared to the sacred gift of trust we've been given. Your life is a sacred trust: your most valuable possession, don't waste it, value it! Life isn't meant for the pursuit of pleasures, but for the pursuit of purpose.

THE TRUE MEASURE OF LIFE

Some years ago, I wrote two wonderful books on this same subject of life which I strongly recommend you get a copy for yourself and anyone you love. They are titled: **"Time Is Life"** and **"Life Is Predictable."** Just the thought of these books alone causes a stir in me. The fact that "Time is Life," and "Life is Predictable" cannot be over-emphasized. I wish I could say more now on these highly essential subjects as well, but let's keep on track with our present truth.

Nonetheless, time is life. Life is measured by what you accomplish with a given frame of time. Time is designed to measure life. Every living thing has a time span: a period designated for its existence, and all its accomplishments falls within its period of life or existence. Now, this includes man, animals, plants and all forms of life even microscopic organisms. Of all creatures, man is the only one with the ability to decide what he or she chooses to accomplish. In other words you have the power of choice to accomplish whatever you desire to within a given space of time. On the opposite, you can choose to live by default: taking life the way it comes to you, which only ends in a severe form of mediocrity and failure. Imagine a football team of players that chooses not to strike nor defend in a match against another team, the former will definitely loose by a default. You are responsible for taking charge of your life and deciding the direction you want to head, and you do so by following the guiding light of God's Word.

Usually, on the tombstone of deceased folks, what you see are two dates separated by a hyphen, besides their names and a little epitaph in their honour. That hyphen as we know defines the time frame or duration of their life's journey. It signifies all they've accomplished during their lifetime or earthly sojourn. Indeed life is a journey.

Take for instance when you're filling a form or submitting an application for a job, a little history of your past and present is also requested for in various ways. It could be an inquiry as to when you were born, when you completed Secondary education, or attended College and so on. What's the purpose of the details? Time, Time is Life. The employer is interested in knowing what has been happening in your life within those periods of time; what purpose were you pursuing at such and such a given time. Is it connected with or relevant to the job you are applying for? In the same way you are to live every day of your life in pursuit of the singular purpose and reason you were born. All your abilities, talents, energies, resources and time must be purposefully directed towards living out the purpose of your life.

All of our lives depend on time, and our ability to discern time is essential in maximizing the opportunities that will come our way and our potentials as well

Your value of life is reflected on how wisely you invest each day. Wasted days culminate in wasted years and lifetime. We are to value each day. We are to number our days, not just months or years:

So teach us to number our days, that we may gain a heart of wisdom.

Psalm 90:12

This prayer of the great prophet of God, Moses, written more two thousand years ago should re-awaken our hearts to the all-important purpose of valuing our time, because time is life. You can't afford to spend your time in pursuit of trivial issues or things that contribute in no way to the purpose of your existence. You need to break down your time from years into months, from months into weeks, from weeks into days, from days into hours, from hours into minutes and even seconds, in order to ensure that you keep track of time in carrying out activities that line up with what you are here on earth to accomplish. Soon your time would be up, as it is the lot of all men, but before then, you need to exercise a consciousness towards reaching the goals and dreams for which you were born. You're here to fulfill definite purposes and time is one of the greatest resources the Creator has given you for this sole aim. Therefore, guard and treasure your time. Time is life. Your time is your life; thus, to waste time is to waste life. To misuse time is to misuse life. To value time is to value life. Therefore, have a deadline for every set goal. Have a program for every day with a specific time frame for every event of the day. Be purposeful with your time because time is life.

LIFE IS A GIFT OF TRUST

"I AM INDEBTED TO MY FATHER FOR LIVING, BUT TO MY TEACHER FOR LIVING WELL."

ALEXANDER THE GREAT

The great Alexander said he is indebted to his teacher for living well. It's not enough to stay alive but to maximize the life you have. One of the major truths about life I would love to emphasize on is the fact that life is a gift, a gift of trust. You didn't produce, manufacture or create your life; it was originally bestowed upon you, by God: the Creator and Source of life. Life is a gift; a most treasured gift to be maximized and well lived. It is to be lived in gratitude to God who gave it to us; our forebears through whom we came into being, and those who helped us on our journey of life.

You came into being because God wants you here at this time, to bring forth solutions that answer specifically to the throes of humanity. Life really is the course of one's existence that brings answers, value and solutions to the throes of humanity.

Your life is a gift of sacred trust, a treasured gift you've been entrusted with to invest wisely in bringing solutions to your world. How you were born doesn't matter, how you came into the world is not an issue. You are here now, so it is time to live and live your best because you've got only one shot. Even if your parents told you that they didn't want you, it's too late. God wanted you. He needed you; that's the reason He gave you the gift of life. You have a great purpose to carry out in His plan for humanity, and you must let nothing stop you. Maximize the gift of life; develop yourself and grow your potentials for a successful living.

Orison Swett Marden described a successful person by saying: *"He was born mud and died a marble."*

Don't die the same way you were born. Don't die as a mud, become a marble. Let the treasures of life in you rise to the surface; let the value and essence of your existence propel you into the fullness of your purpose. Develop yourself. Fulfill your purpose. It is often said that great treasures and talents are often in the graveyard. Let your story be different. Do not go back to dust with treasures you should have released to impact your generation.

Have you come across the story of Alexander Solzhenitsyn, the Russian novelist and Nobel Prize winner who was an outspoken critic of the Soviet Union and communism? He was thrown into prison for criticizing Joseph Stalin. He went into prison as an atheist but came out as a believer, and his horrifying experience didn't make him bitter as expected. Rather, he turned out to be grateful for the development of his faith in God and strengthening of his character.

> "THE OBJECT OF LIFE IS NOT PROSPERING AS I HAD GROWN UP BELIEVING, BUT THE MATURING OF THE SOUL."
>
> ALEXANDER SOLZHENITSYN

Indeed the purpose of life is not prosperity. The purpose of life isn't the accumulation of wealth and riches; neither is it the acquisition of wisdom or power. It is the maturation of your soul and use of your potential in service of humanity.

No wonder Alexander ended up winning the Pulitzer Prize. His character was moulded through the difficult experiences he garnered and lessons he learnt along the way. He had become marble and not just mud - a transformed person in totality. He allowed himself to be transformed into an agent of national transformation, using his painful experience to help others and improve his nation. He understood the essence of disregarding the bitterness of the past in order to influence lives positively with the essential values of life such as forgiveness, kindness, and mercy.

Life is a gift of trust, and it's your sole responsibility today to improve yourself daily and develop your potential in order to bring value to your world at large. Make great efforts to bring value to those you meet daily and the society you live in, because not only is your life a gift of trust, but you as well are a gift to the world.

THE ORIGIN AND SOURCE OF LIFE

Before closing this chapter, it's highly essential that we be well acquainted with the true Source of life. It's vital to note that life isn't an accident or product of fate. We aren't here by mere chance. The world isn't a product of accident or coincidence. If it were so, I would say that was a very big, organized and well planned out accident or coincidence, but no. We are here by the plan of the Creator of the Universe. You're here on earth at this time because God: the Giver and Source of life choose to give you life and bring you into this world.

Even if your parents were expecting a baby, they didn't know it was you in particular. But God who formed you in your mother's womb and gave you life before you were born knew you in advance. Your purpose was designed before your birth by the Creator-God, who is the Source of life.

That is the reason Jesus said: *"I am the Way, the Truth and the Life, no man comes to the Father except through Me."* He is the Way to the Source of Life; He is the Truth about life and He is Life – the very essence of Life. In fact life truly and fully begins when you receive Jesus Christ as your personal Lord and Saviour: embracing His forgiveness of sin and His free gift of eternal life that comes through His sacrificial death for our sins and resurrection to life for our justification. He died for your sins and God raised Him to life for your justification.

If you desire to receive His free gift of salvation, kindly open the last page of this book, and pray the sinner's prayer of salvation. When you do this, then life really begins.

GOLDEN NUGGETS

1. When you understand the truth, your journey of life becomes purpose-driven.

2. Life is an opportunity that comes only once; therefore make the most of every opportunity that comes your way.

3. Life is more than the wisdom we pursue, more than the power we crave for, more than all the wealth and riches money can buy.

4. Investing in yourself is one of the ways of showing the value you place on the gift of life.

5. Life is measured by what you have accomplished within a given frame of time.

6. Your value of life is reflected on how wisely you invest each day.

7. Life isn't an accident or product of fate – God chose to give you life.

8. Life really is the course of one's existence that brings answer, value and solution to the throes of humanity.

CHAPTER 2

UNDERSTANDING THE PURPOSE OF LIFE

"THE PURPOSE OF HUMAN LIFE IS TO SERVE, AND TO SHOW COMPASSION AND THE WILL TO HELP OTHERS."

ALBERT SCHWEITZER

Understanding the purpose of life is such a vital subject for every living human person. So many who are alive today are completely clueless regarding the purpose of life, while others simply go through the motions of life based on the patterns set by others, even when such are wrong and faulty to live by.

Have you ever stopped to ask yourself *"What is the purpose of life? Why am I alive on earth today?"* Asking the right questions is absolutely essential in obtaining answers that will bring about all-round transformation. You need to know the reason for living; otherwise life ceases to have a reason.

No reasonable hunter takes a shot into an empty space without a definite reason or defined target. No farmer sows seeds on his farm without a definite expectation of reaping a harvest. In the same way, you need to discover concretely and pursue purposefully your reason for being alive on the planet today. Since life is only a one-time experience, you must live in such a way that

31

if you look back in retrospect, you'd be glad you really lived and lived out your purpose for being.

No other person has a greater responsibility for living your life to the best than you do. Every other person in life starting from your parents, forbears, teachers, mentors are simply given to guide and counsel you. But the onus lies entirely on you to discover, acknowledge and pursue your purpose in life. Nobody can do this for you, except you. And long after you're gone, it is the purpose you lived for that would remain.

Moreover, every life well lived has always been based on an accurate understanding of one's purpose and a deliberate pursuit of that purpose. You need to live life with purpose. You need to wake up each morning with a consciousness that you are here on earth to solve a problem; that you have a mission and an assignment in life.

If the Creator who made this great Universe created everything to solve a problem, it sure implies you too are here to meet a need that either existed before you were born or God knew will be in existence during your life-time. You are here for a reason!

"THE PURPOSE OF LIFE IS TO LIVE A LIFE OF PURPOSE."

RICHARD LEIDER

Everything created by God exist to fulfill a definite purpose. There is a definite purpose for your life; a reason for your existence at this very moment. You aren't a product of chance. God who created you brought you into the earth for such a time as this. There is a clear-cut agenda for you to fulfill on earth, a specific assignment carved out to suit the specifics of your unique person-ality. You aren't here by accident; you're here for a reason, and I'm going to be sharing with you the essence for your being alive today.

It is an established fact that where purpose is unknown abuse is inevitable. The abuse of life is so tangible all over the world, where many misuse life due to the ignorance of purpose or difficult experiences they faced early in life.

THE COST OF IGNORANCE

"EVIL ACTIONS ARE THE RESULT OF IGNORANCE."

PLATO

Ignorance is so expensive. It is the timeworn mystery behind the terrors and evils that had bedevilled our society through the years.

Have you ever heard people say: *what you don't know can hurt you*? It is absolutely true, especially when it comes to this all important subject of understanding your purpose in life. A person who is ignorant of his purpose in life will constitute not only a misfortune, not only to himself, but a terror to others and the society at large. The causalities of life are nothing short of men driven without purpose. A man with a poor understanding of purpose is like an inexperienced driver on a highway, speeding on with no caution, speed limits or destina-tion in mind. That's an accident going somewhere to happen. No wonder the news channels and daily tabloids are never devoid of tragic disasters and with increasing suicidal and homicide rates.

The flood of ignorance endangers the very foundation of life and civilization. It remains the undeniable reason for the hideous corruption, crimes and prevalent visage of evil plaguing our society today. Ignorance kills and it's a killer too. It is so contagious. Though we live in an information age, many are still ignorant of their life's purpose. Being ignorant of your purpose in life is absolutely dangerous; it is too expensive to afford.

According to Webster's Dictionary, ignorance is either "a lack of experience or knowledge" or "the state of being uninformed." But I believe ignorance isn't a mere absence of essential knowledge, but a turning away from the truth of life, a deliberate rejection of available truth:

"My people are destroyed for lack of knowledge. Because you have rejected knowledge, I also will reject you from being priest for Me; Because you have forgotten the law of your God, I also will forget your children."

Hosea 4:6

It's one thing to know your purpose in life; it's another thing entirely to commit yourself towards fulfilling that reason for your being. You are entirely responsible for fulfilling the purpose of your life. It will not happen accidentally or passively; it requires your whole-hearted commitment and unswerving persistence in discovering and fulfilling it.

Throughout history, ignorance has destroyed uncountable number of lives. Think about the millions of lives lost in selfish pursuit of wealth with no thought for others; lives lost through senseless wars orchestrated by leaders of nations; innocent children lost because people couldn't afford the bare necessities of life. It is vividly clear that we must fight this pandemic of ignorance otherwise life would continue to be an unfulfilled journey of sorrows with no defined destination.

Life on earth is a one-time opportunity. You can only live once, thus it's highly essential to have a good understanding of your purpose on earth so that you can live out your existence in a purpose-driven manner. Purpose can never be created; it is only to be discovered. Being ignorant of your purpose in life is not an excuse. You ought to know and live out your reason for being. Successful people are simply those who have discovered their purpose and are daily taking steps towards fulfilling it. When you understand your purpose for living, you will take charge of your life and set realistic goals. You will make plans for personal growth and develop the skills necessary to be proficient in your area of calling. You will live a life of commitments and be intentional in your pursuits because you have the blueprints.

Life is not just to be lived for selfish gains. It isn't just about what you feel like doing but rather what has to be done. People are being told that your purpose in life lies in your greatest interest, that thing that makes you happy. No. life is more than selfish interest. Someone who doesn't understand purpose may not understand how to fulfill purpose with passion. Someone said, 'my greatest interest is to sit down and watch different football matches'. So, he sits down all day to watch football. Is he fulfilling purpose? He is definitely not doing so.

"THE PURPOSE OF LIFE IS NOT TO BE HAPPY. IT IS TO BE USEFUL, TO BE HONOURABLE, TO BE COMPASSIONATE, AND TO HAVE IT MAKE SOME DIFFERENCE THAT YOU HAVE LIVED AND LIVED WELL."

RALPH WALDO EMERSON

Life is to be lived to make a difference in your world. The Bible says in Jude 22 that we should have compassion and make a difference.

Most of the problems thronging our society today are due to the prevalence of ignorance and our failure to rightly apply the knowledge we've garnered towards bringing about positive changes.

Take for instance there was a time when the scientific cure for malaria was unknown worldwide. Can you imagine that today? And so many white missionaries who came to the African continent died here because of the disease, while some others had to return home immediately, in terrible sick condition. Not only was the African continent plagued by this horrifying illness, even the American continent then was seriously affected too, until a cure was found and applied. Knowledge had come, the understanding of what caused the illness was discovered and the cure was applied. Thus, was malaria completed eradicated from the United States between 1947-1951. Despite the availability of cure, sadly today, several thousands of children in our own African continent die daily due to this same ailment of which the cure has already been discovered, simply because it hasn't been made sufficiently available to all and prevent measures applied appropriately.

Yet we have lot of money pumped into this project yearly in our country, lot of medical practitioners are trained for this. If it happened for United States, it can happen for Nigeria and many other African countries. The challenge is for us to rise up to a total commitment to our purpose.

Not only must you discover your purpose in life, you need to be very committed and conscientious in applying it otherwise you would still be a victim of your own ignorance.

DISCOVERING YOUR PURPOSE IN LIFE

"YOU WERE PUT ON THIS EARTH TO ACHIEVE YOUR GREATEST SELF, TO LIVE OUT YOUR PURPOSE, AND TO DO IT COURAGEOUSLY."

DR STEVE MARABOLI

Everything that God created has a specific function and purpose - and that includes you. God gave you life and certain unique abilities for a reason. If you haven't discovered what that purpose is, I encourage you to begin to do so, because the discovery of your purpose is the starting point of success, greatness and fulfillment in life.

There was a time in life I thought I was good for nothing and would amount to nothing. Unfortunately, this is how a lot of people think of themselves today, and thus end up living in misery and misfortune. This also accounts for the reason many resort to crime, prostitution, homicide, alcoholism and drug addiction as a way to cover up the shame and emptiness they feel inside.

A lady who offers her body for sex to men in exchange for money doesn't understand the value of her life. She undervalues herself and lives in a state of total emptiness.

What about the man who takes a gun, breaks into peoples' houses at night to steal and kill? If only he discovered the real reason for being alive and the value of the human life, his success would be enviable without such evil.

The truth about life is that you are valuable to God, so valuable that He gave His only begotten Son to save you from sin. You're of great value in God's sight and carry within a great purpose in life; you're good for something! No matter the bitter experiences you had in the past, you need to recognize that the past is gone and all you have today is the present and future. Yesterday is gone, so let it go! You have value, therefore add value to others. You need to deliberately look away from any past experience that undervalues your self-worth and live today and every other day as your new beginning, because, there is a purpose for your life. There are tasks that the Creator has assigned for you to undertake, and if you don't do them, they may never be done. Even if someone else did them, they could never do it exactly like you, because there is only one "you" in the whole world. You are the first and last you God will ever have and this world will ever see. So be the best of you! Don't waste your life. Invest your life.

There are people God has planned for you to meet, and be a blessing to, and if you don't meet them, they might miss out on that blessing, and you too would miss out fulfilling purpose. There are places He's planned for you to go to bring solution in a time of desperate need. There are problems He created you to solve; answers He designed for you to bring. You are here for a definite reason; a reason that brings meaning to the lives of others.

You are the answer to the problems in your society. You are the saviour your nation needs. Stop looking for politicians who can solve the societal ills of today; stand up and bring life to your own world. You are the answer!

Just like salt brings out meaning in every cooking, you are the salt of the earth, the salt of your office or industry; the salt of your school or institution; the salt of your society or state. You've been sent by the Creator to bring meaning to the lives of many in this world. You're born to make a difference. In the same way salt doesn't exist for itself, you do not exist for yourself. Your life is designed to bring good to others and preserve your society from decay. Don't remain passive, rise up and influence your world; transform your society and restore hope to the hopeless.

Your optimum fulfillment will emerge from living out your real purpose, doing what you were created to do on earth.

THE MEANING OF LIFE

"THE MEANING OF LIFE IS TO FIND YOUR GIFT. THE PURPOSE OF LIFE IS TO GIVE IT AWAY."

PABLOPICASSO

39

When you begin solving problems close to where you are and improving yourself daily through an effective self-education program, your mind will be opened to the real purpose for your being. God designed you with a definite purpose in mind; He created you so you can solve problems on earth. You are here to bring solutions; you are God's answer to your world. Every detail of your existence including: your family, nationality, gender, education, experiences, even challenges and difficulties were designed not to stop you, but point you to the sole purpose of life. You must be intentional in your discovery and pursuit of your purpose in life.

Moreover, your purpose in life could be connected with your areas of gifting or passion. When you identify your areas of gifting or talent, you're to walk on developing them in solving problems where you are.

"IF YOU CAN'T FIGURE OUT YOUR PURPOSE, FIGURE OUT YOUR PASSION. FOR YOUR PASSION WILL LEAD RIGHT INTO YOUR PURPOSE."

BISHOP T. D. JAKES

I've always loved to say that one's purpose is where his pain and passion intersects; this is from my personal experience. When I came into the city of Kiev, after my years of University education in Belarus, my heart was aflame for the city, I felt an irresistible sense of responsibility regarding the state of the land, an unbreakable love for the people yet angry passion for the spiritual bondage they were experiencing. It was so real and profound that I couldn't hold back my tears as I drove round the city and found myself praying that God would help me make a life-transforming difference in this place. I had a burning passion to restore dignity to these lovely people and moral value to their beloved society. I knew the answer wasn't in the hands of the politicians, but in my hands, because I came to understand that I was a partner with God in removing the thorns that plague the society and her citizenry, and bring the Kingdom of God to the hearts of men and their society in totality. This was my purpose, and still is. I felt the people's pain; I could identify with them. I believe this was how Moses felt for his people that prompted him to take the wrong step of killing an Egyptian who was oppressing an Israelite. His love for his people and identification with their suffering was almost unbearable and uncontrollable that ended up taking a risky step that could have cost his life and calling. So, God had to retrain and re-educate him in a desert to develop a shepherd's heart in him, because that's what was needed for the task of delivering over three million Jews from the hand of Pharaoh, the Egyptian leader and lead them into their promise land.

I want to ask you: have you discovered your purpose in life yet? Do you have a burning desire to meet a need or solve a problem in your society? What's your hobby or area of passion? Do you have an insatiable desire to transform your society or meet a need in your community? What do you have a driving passion for and love to accomplish? It may be that God has called you to deal with those issues with your talents and time.

Discovering your purpose in life is your ultimate responsibility and you need to search deeply inwards and cooperate with God in discovering your purpose.

God doesn't want you to be ignorant of your primary assignment in life. That's the reason He stated it out in the scripture as referenced below:

"This is what the Lord says: "Let not the wise boast of their wisdom or the strong boast of their strength or the rich boast of their riches, but let the one who boasts boast about this: that they have the understanding to know me, that I am the Lord, who exercises kindness, justice and righteousness on earth, for in these I delight, "declares the Lord."

Jeremiah 9:23-24

In other words, the essential purpose of life isn't the acquisition of wisdom, riches or strength. Making money, getting married, being educated and employed isn't the primary aim for existence. These are just means to that end. This shouldn't be your primary pursuit and reason for living. Rather, these efforts should be purposefully tailored towards fulfilling your purpose. That means the central purpose of all you do: education, marriage, financial success etc. should be targeted at fulfilling your purpose in life. Anything besides this is simply a waste of time and energy.

I feel so sad when I hear of politicians who misappropriate their nation's income, stealing public funds, and channeling them into their private bank account in other foreign nations. I wish to God they understood the purpose of life isn't to accumulate riches especially through corrupt means. All forms of cheating is liable to shame and failure. These nefarious deeds constitute an abuse of life, and abuse inevitably results in loss. Nobody will ever take his wealth and riches with him when leaving this world. When your time is up, all that would be left of you is the purpose for which you lived, because purpose never dies. Wealth will end one day, wisdom could fail and strength could fade out with time, but purpose never dies. It speaks through all ages and dispensations. Your purpose in life is the most essential reason for your existence. It is the reason you are here. When you stop fulfilling purpose; you stop living. Those who are alive today and aren't fulfilling their purpose of life are merely existing; not living. To live is to fulfill purpose; the purpose of life! To live fulfilling purpose is a choice you must make and pursue daily no matter the cost.

THE TRUE ESSENCE OF LIFE

"WITHOUT GOD, LIFE HAS NO PURPOSE, AND WITHOUT PURPOSE, LIFE HAS NO MEANING. WITHOUT MEANING, LIFE HAS NO SIGNIFICANCE OR HOPE."

RICK WARREN

The true essence of life is having an accurate understanding of God and exercising kindness, justice and righteousness in your dealings with people. That is the primary purpose of life on earth! This should be your guiding light in living a purpose-driven life on earth.

Without the accurate knowledge of God, life would be misunderstood and purpose frustrated. Take for instance the Islamic extremists who embark on suicide

43

bombings and slaughter of fellow human beings in the name of their religion! To destroy another human life just because he differs from your religious views is both wicked and devilish. It's a most terrible consequence of being indoctrinated with an inaccurate knowledge of God. Think about the thousands of individuals, families and professionals that were lost during the 9/11 attack. That was a result of widespread religious ignorance of the accurate knowledge of God passed.

I've even heard that in some places before thieves embark on armed robbery, they get together in prayer and fasting for a successful mission. What else could be farther from the truth? Is this an extreme expression of ignorance of the personality and values of God? Killing, stealing, cheating and committing various atrocities in the name of God is simply a reflection of the high level of ignorance prevalent in our society today.

I can never over-emphasize the extensive value of knowing God personally. You can't depend entirely on your grandmother's stories of Him or what someone else has said, you need to discover Him in the pages of the Bible. You need to have a personal revelation and understanding of your Creator founded on the light of His word as contained in the Holy Bible, as any knowledge of Him contrary to the written scriptures is both false and misleading.

Having the right and accurate knowledge of God is the starting point in understanding your purpose in life, because the more you know God, the more you discover yourself in Him.

It's quite unfortunate and disheartening for some folks who though, have been attending Church meetings most of their lives and have continued to remain trapped in a web of chronic ignorance on the essential truths regarding the person of God and values of the Kingdom, thus, misrepresenting His person and values in the society. You need to take absolute responsibility for knowing God and living the quality of life He's purposed for you. You need to take charge of your life.

"A LIFE WITHOUT CAUSE IS A LIFE WITHOUT EFFECT."

PAULO COELHO

The direction you lead to in life will determine the impact you will make. The essential truth about the primary purpose of life is stated repeatedly all through scriptures in various ways:

"He has shown you, O man, what is good; and what does the LORD require of you but to do justly, to love mercy, and to walk humbly with your God?"

Micah 6:8

If you observe this verse of scripture is consistent with the previous one we quoted from Jeremiah 9:23-24, which declares that the purpose of life is to know God, exercise kindness, justice and righteousness. But here it puts it slightly differently with the same truth repeated: *"to do justly, love mercy and walk humbly with thy God."* To do justly is just the same as exercising justice; to love mercy equates exercising kindness, and to walk humbly with your God is synonymous to exercising righteousness. Thus, the truth about the purpose of life is well emphasized in the scriptures. That means, we are to live our lives in a manner that projects the virtues of justice, kindness and righteousness in our all our dealings with men. This is the true essence of life!

GOLDEN NUGGETS

1. Every life well lived has always been based on an accurate understanding of one's purpose and a deliberate pursuit of that purpose.

2. There is a clear-cut agenda for you to fulfill on earth, a specific assignment carved out to suit the specifics of your unique personality.

3. Not only must you discover your purpose in life, you need to be very committed and conscientious in applying it. Otherwise, you will be a victim of your own ignorance.

4. In the same way salt doesn't exist for itself, you do not exist for yourself rather for a purpose.

5. Your purpose in life is usually connected to your areas of gifting or passion.

6. When you stop fulfilling purpose, you stop living and are merely existing.

7. Having the right and accurate knowledge of God is the starting point in understanding your purpose in life.

CHAPTER 3

DEADLY DISTRACTIONS
OF LIFE

"FOCUS IS OFTEN A MATTER OF DECIDING
WHAT THINGS YOU'RE NOT GOING TO DO."

JOHN CARMACK

In life we all are faced with various forms of distractions designed to keep us from reaching our goals, accomplishing our set tasks and becoming the person we've always desired to be. Sometimes, our distractions could even appear so simple and harmless, but when we reflect on how much time of our lives we devote to these distractions, we may quickly come to terms with how off-track we really are and distracted from the true essence of life.

Life is a journey, and being on track is so important in fulfilling the essence of your being. You must preserve your mind from the distractions of life otherwise you could become a victim of those very things that steal away your attention and focus. The choice to be intentional in overcoming the various distractions of life actually lies in your hands. You must fight to gain control of your attention and stay away from the deadly diversions on the journey of life.

When Joshua, the protégé of Moses assumed leadership of the Israelite nation, he was charged with the immense task of leading his nation into the Promised

Land and dividing the inheritance among the various tribes, a task his boss undertook at the beginning but couldn't complete. Among the words of instructions and counsel given to him by the Lord God on how to accomplish this all-important goal was the caution on avoiding distractions. If this great leader was to succeed in life and in his assignment, distractions were to be identified and seriously avoided.

"Only be strong and very courageous, that you may observe to do according to all the law which Moses My servant commanded you; do not turn from it to the right hand or to the left, that you may prosper wherever you go."

Joshua 1:7

This was the very charge the Lord God gave to Joshua: *"...do not turn from it to the right hand or to the left, that you may prosper wherever you go."*

In other words, to succeed, you must identify the goal of life, your purpose for living, which we did in the previous chapter, then stick to it, not turning aside from it. Refuse to be distracted or diverted from the right trail and pathway of life, because there are other ways that seem right, but they all end in destruction and painful regrets. If you want to fulfill your days on earth, let your life be a journey of well-defined purpose and stay clear from the deadly distractions and traps of life.

It's very easy to allow yourself to be distracted, and get involved in other interesting endeavours, but it takes a lot of courage, maturity and discipline of mind, to constantly acknowledge one's goal, strive for it, and look away from all forms of distractions.

THE TRUTH BEHIND DISTRACTION

So many today are unwittingly caught up in a vicious cycle of distractions. They've abandoned their goals, neglected their purposes, ignored their values and breached their plans for success in life.

Nobody sets out with a plan to divert from the blueprints of life, but we do so when we fail to identify our purpose for living, committing ourselves wholly to them and at the same time equally and honestly admitting what constitutes or could be a real source of distraction and avoiding them. You need to be honest with yourself if you will truly overcome the distractions and traps of life, and move on towards the reality of reaching your dreams and purpose for living.

The truth about most distractions in life is they always seem so appealing and interesting. The fact is they don't stop you from moving, but are sure diversions from your designated route. Moreover, distractions are mostly attractive and appear interesting, but in the real sense are empty and void of the real substance that makes life worth living. Take for instance, the social media or Television is a good platform for expressing your purpose and values, but it could also be a real source of distraction if not handled with caution. It could really consume your time and attention, and diverting your focus from what you were supposed to do. Today, so many youngsters spend several hours of their day on Facebook, Whatsapp, Twitter etc., whiling away their youthful vigour and life on nothing but mindless chats, not considering that a waste of time is a waste of life. This ends in giving out very little of the great treasures in you to your world.

All distractions are designed to hinder you from reaching your desired goals or pursue your purpose. Any distraction you give you attention will not only consume your time, but consume your life. It's high time we applied wisdom in this area to avoid all that undermines the essence for which we are alive today.

Before considering certain factors that could allure and distract our attention from the main essence for living, I would like to stress that these distractions have become traps into which many great people have fallen victims. Therefore, you need to beware of them and keep your guard lest you too be carried away in the wrong pursuit and waste the very essence for which the Creator brought you into this world.

If you allow yourself to be trapped by these enticing distractions, life would lose its sense of meaning, and you could end up becoming very unserious minded about life and the main reason you're alive on earth. It's so important you don't fall into these traps, rather, identify them and overcome them. Since there are no prior preparations for living before one is born, we need to get armed with wisdom as we journey on so we don't caught up as victims but victors in the endeavours of life.

So put on your seat belts as we now explore what these traps of life really are, that has lured many into giving their lives in exchange for, and how to decipher them and overcome them.

Are you ready?

THREE DEADLY TRAPS

"This is what the Lord says: "Let not the wise boast of their wisdom or the strong boast of their strength or the rich boast of their riches, but let the one who boasts boast about this: that they have the understanding to know me, that I am the Lord, who exercises kindness, justice and righteousness on earth, for in these I delight, declares the Lord."

Jeremiah 9:23-24

God's Word is and forever remains the number one and most reliable source on the matters of life. It reveals to us, not only the purpose of life, but factors that could destroy the very reason for which we live, if care isn't taken. Let's revert to our original text which unveils this vital information regarding these lethal traps that must be avoided.

According to the scripture we read, the big three distractions of life include: Wisdom, Power and Riches. Wisdom, Power and Riches are all good and absolutely essential for life on earth. We value them, we need them, but we aren't supposed to give our lives in exchange for these. They shouldn't be your reason for living. That's because they constitute a force capable of misleading anyone away from the principal purpose of life. They are to be tools for life, not the purpose for living.

I would still love to succinctly and emphatically state here that there is nothing wrong with these three factors stated above. There's nothing wrong with wisdom, power and riches. Everyone needs wisdom to deal rightly in the affairs of life, every individual needs power to execute his purpose for living and we all need riches to enjoy our lives and help others along the way.

But the terrible mistake many indulge in is by devoting their entire lives in the pursuit of any or one of these factors, at the expense of their primary purpose or calling in life. In as much as these factors are all needed for our journey of life, they shouldn't become your central focus, driving force or motive for living. In other words, you shouldn't live mainly for the acquisition of wisdom, power or wealth. These shouldn't be reason for your living, though they are quite essential in the fulfillment your purpose of in life.

Let's take for instance wealth or money. It is true that money has seductive power. If you don't believe that, step out early one morning on the streets by 7am and observe to see how many people are rushing to get to their offices on time. If you're chanced, kindly ask one of them why he is so much in a haste to get to work on time, is it merely because they are in love with the concept of work, offering goods and services to humanity; or is it primarily because of the value they obtain on the pay cheque or cash flow that gets into the account by month's end? I'm sure you'd get the right answer.

All over the world, people are committing several hours to their work, all in the bid to make ends meet, or heighten their prosperity and wealth. Unfortunately, where many miss the mark is when the pursuit of riches becomes the primary reason for their living. Life is not about making money, neither is it about wielding influ-

DEADLY DISTRACTIONS OF LIFE

ence or power. It isn't about an endless acquisition of knowledge and wisdom.

The purpose of life isn't to make money or become extremely rich. This dire misunderstanding of the purpose of life has been the root cause behind the corrupt financial practices that has led many nations, including ours into a degenerated state of economic recession and heightened poverty level, where many kill and destroy innocent lives all for the sake of wealth acquisition or to gain a political office. Knowing fully well, that one day they die and leave all those wealth, and political power to another, and their time of departure is uncertain, such makes vanity of life!

Life is all about God; it's all about discovering and fulfilling His purpose for your being. It's all about spreading His kingdom on earth by upholding His values of kindness, justice, and righteousness in the various spheres of human endeavours. Life is all about purpose. Let this be your singular focus and reason for living.

Dangers Behind these Allurements

If you were brought into a treasure house full of diamonds, gold and money, and were asked to deny the existence of God or to act contrary to your moral values, what would be your reaction, especially if it were a time you were in dire need of that money?

Would you be tempted to compromise your values in order to achieve your desire, or maintain a solid front against that which is wrong?

So many are in this situation today, and it reminds me of a certain young man who was offered a job in a private firm right after his University education. After some years of working there and excelling in his duties, he was required of his superiors to come short on the quality of the products they were offering without any formal information to their consumers. Being a true Christian with an understanding of the kingdom values, he refused to play to their tune and maintained his integrity at the expense of losing his job. Eventually, this Company began to experience losses, and folded up but God granted this believer a better opportunity. He was glad at the end of the day that he did what was right, in exercising kindness, justice and righteousness, even when it cost him his career, and God was faithful.

It pays to do what is right when others are letting down their guard. It pays to maintain your integrity even when doing what is right isn't popular. We are here on earth, not for ourselves but for God - to spread the principles and values of His kingdom in all spheres of our society. We are actually His ambassadors: representing the interest of His Kingdom on earth. So be conscious of who you are and why you're here.

I was deeply touched when I read a newspaper story of a certain student who secured admission into the University of Ilorin, Kwara State, Nigeria for a course of his choice. After he obtained a successful placement and resumed his academics program, along the way, he heard the Gospel of the Kingdom and surrendered his life to Christ. Then he recalled clearly, that he cheated his way through the exams to secure his most prized admission. In other words, his University placement wasn't based on the merits of his own efforts, but through exam malpractice. Thus, in a bid to make things right, he wrote a letter addressed to the University authorities, to confess his wrong doing and request a forfeiting of his admission because of his faith in Jesus and value for the Kingdom. This young chap turned down his admission, what thousands of youths all over this country are struggling to obtain, and returned to re-sit the West African Secondary School Certificate Exams. What a kingdom spirit and value of the truth. These are the type of folks the world needs: men of character and value.

I know many would have simply prayed: "O God, please forgive me" and moved on, but not this young believer, who sought to please God and understood that life is not about what we achieve, but how right we live in the sight of God.

Unfortunately, many acclaimed believers pass their exams through malpractice today, when they assume public offices, they continue in their corrupt lifestyle by stealing public funds. Some even go the extra mile of cheating on their spouses with an unrepentant heart, ignoring the values of life. All these bring abuse on the key matters of life. We need to understand the Kingdom and give our lives for it.

There's an incidence that keeps re-occurring in Higher Institutions all across our nation. A situation where a lecturer intentional fails a female student offering his course, or delays her academic program until she succumbs to his devilish request for sex. And if she refuses, he makes sure she makes no progress academically as long as he is concerned. Quite unfortunate! In most cases, these so-called lecturers are married men with children about the same ages of young ladies whose lives and future they frustrate and endanger, at the expense of their lustful desires. Thus using his power or authority to intimidate the innocent and violate their free will against their moral values.

The dangers that result when we make our pursuit of wisdom, power or wealth could be very disastrous. These distractions can inundate one aggressively and cause great addictions.

GET FREE FROM THEM

The secret behind King Solomon's early success in life was founded in his passion to know God and uphold virtues of justice, kindness and righteousness during his reign as king in his dealings with his people. The Bible says that He loved the Lord. Sadly today, the reason many go to church these days is connected to their selfish desires or egocentric expectations of having the Lord bless them, and when they don't find their expectations fulfilled immediately, they draw back on their spiritual commitments. This clearly denotes that they don't love God or desire His knowledge which is the key purpose of life. God is not their primary interest, neither is the knowledge of His values and kingdom principles. Their primary pursuit is selfish aggrandizement and ambitions. Money and power is their goal. This shouldn't be so. We need to get our priorities straight. We are to seek first God's kingdom and His righteousness; then all other things will be added to us. Your primary pursuit in life should be the spread of the knowledge of His kingdom in your world.

This was the burning desire of Solomon even before he became king. That explains why when his brother, Adonijah struggled to usurp the throne and seize the power to become king, he was unperturbed because he understood that the goal of life isn't power or affluence. Even Absalom, when he became power-thirsty, to the extent of chasing his father, King David, out of the throne to exile, eventually ended up defeated, though his army was greater than his father's. . Thus, these brothers who made power their primary pursuit all died in their prime and never lived to fulfill their purpose in life. They didn't have to seat on a throne in order to fulfill their purpose. What they needed first was to make God and the spread of His Kingdom their priority.

"But seek first the Kingdom of God and his righteousness and all these things shall be added unto you."

Matthew 6:33

In his earliest moments as King, Solomon was always available in God's presence, panting to know Him and how to spread His kingdom in the affairs of men. His passion was so tangible that he kept showing up at the temple to offer burnt offerings until he caught God's attention in an indelible way. God appeared to him in a dream asking him what his heart desire was.

Have you ever wondered, if God came to visit you and asked you what you wanted Him to do for you? For some folks I'm sure they will get a lengthy prayer list of all sorts of request, especially the death of their enemies.

For Solomon, his heart was set on the Kingdom. His heart was set on the very desires of God. His passion and hunger were focused on the very same things God wanted; he was in sync with God. Thus, when he made his request known, the Lord was so pleased.

It's important to know that God isn't our errand boy or servant we throw all kinds of requests at. He is our Master, Creator and Lord God. We are to do His biddings, and carry out His glorious will, and the spread of the Kingdom is His number one desire. This was Solomon's perspective.

You need the right perspective: a kingdom mindset in order not to fall victim in life and be carried by the worldly proofs of success. Having many cars, houses and lots of money and a good paying job isn't the primary goal of life. The Kingdom is! Your value in life isn't based on our material valuables, but on Kingdom values.

King Solomon had set his priorities straight: it was God first and His kingdom. Thus when he presented his request to God, his passion for the Kingdom was evidently portrayed:

> **At Gibeon the LORD appeared to Solomon in a dream by night; and God said, Ask! What shall I give you? And Solomon said: You have shown great mercy to Your servant David my father, because he walked before You in truth, in righteousness, and in uprightness of heart with You; You have continued this great kindness for him, and You have given him a son to sit on his throne, as it is this day. Now, O LORD my God, You have made Your servant king instead of my father David, but I am a little child; I do not know how to go out or come in. And Your servant is in the midst of Your people whom You have chosen, a great people, too numerous to be numbered**

or counted. Therefore give to Your servant an understanding heart to judge Your people, that I may discern between good and evil. For who is able to judge this great people of Yours? The speech pleased the Lord, that Solomon had asked this thing. Then God said to him: "Because you have asked this thing, and have not asked long life for yourself, nor have asked riches for yourself, nor have asked the life of your enemies, but have asked for yourself understanding to discern justice, behold, I have done according to your words; see, I have given you a wise and understanding heart, so that there has not been anyone like you before you, nor shall any like you arise after you. And I have also given you what you have not asked: both riches and honor, so that there shall not be anyone like you among the kings all your days.

1 Kings 3:5-13

If you read through this passage carefully, you will observe that the kingdom values of Kindness, Righteousness and Justice are being exemplified in different ways, thus validating these as core ingredients of life.

Moreover, in this discourse between God and Solomon, the humility of this young king was tangible. He humbled himself in the presence of God. It was evident in the manner in his prayer. How important this is today. I wish I could emphasize on how we must learn to humble ourselves before God, becoming as a child before the King of Kings. Get rid of your ego, pride and accomplishments, because before Him these are nothing. He is the Source of every good thing, and what we have, He gave to us. You need to humble yourself in His presence, that's how elevation comes in life.

Now, more importantly is the content of his prayer, his request to God. Solomon asked for one thing: an understanding heart to lead God's people aright in order to fulfill his calling. One simple but wise request!

God was so touched and pleased with this request, that He took notice of the fact that Solomon's desire and request wasn't selfish or egocentric. His request wasn't all about what he wanted; it was all about God wanted. Life isn't all about what we desire; it is all about what God desires. God doesn't exist for us, we exist for God.

Solomon's request was unusual and exceptional. He didn't ask of what others normally would. He didn't request for long life, riches, fame, power, destruction of his enemies, but for understanding to discern justice. He prayed for an understanding heart to do what is right before God.

Did he get it, was his request granted?

More than granted, I would say. God gave him a wise and understanding heart exceeding what his predecessors possessed and successors would. In other words, this man had more wisdom than his father, David, the great King of Israel; he had more wisdom than Moses, the Prophet of God.

I would like to point out here, like we read in scriptures that wisdom wasn't his primary pursuit. He wasn't trying to merely acquire wisdom to surpass others in greatness and become a figure of great renown. Rather, his prayer and desire was to have a heart of understanding to execute the will of God and spread the kingdom on earth. His desire was to have an understanding heart, in other words, a heart that comprehends the will of God and executes His purposes effectively. This was the man's longing.

I admonish you today, to adopt this same mind-set and develop a heart that puts the interest of God's kingdom ahead of yours. Let the agenda of His kingdom come first to you, because as Jesus said and as we see, Solomon obtained all other things others were chasing after. Putting God's interest ahead of yours is the surest way to receiving all other blessings He freely gives.

Thus, God gave Solomon a wise and understanding heart; and in addition, great riches and honour that no King ever had, before him or after him. This is amazing!

The benefits that emerge when God and His kingdom becomes your number one pursuit is dumbfounding and humbling, more than words can describe, and beyond this is the fulfillment you enjoy in your journey of life.

That's the reason I've always endeavoured to ensure my priorities are in the right perspective. Nothing and no one comes before God, not even my lovely Princess, Pastor Bose or my adorable children. It has to be God first; then family, and thirdly, ministry, in that order always, otherwise, I'm in trouble.

GOLDEN NUGGETS

1. You must preserve your mind from distractions of life otherwise you could be a victim of those things that steal away your attention and focus.

2. The truth about most distractions in life is they always seem so appealing and interesting.

3. All distractions are designed to hinder you from reaching your desired goals or pursue of purpose.

4. Three big distractions of life are wisdom, power and riches.

5. You need the right perspectives; a kingdom mindset in order not to fall victim in life and be carried by worldly proofs of success.

6. Your value isn't based on material valuables, but on kingdom values.

7. Life isn't all about what we desire; it is all about what God desires. God doesn't exist for us, we exist for Him.

8. God and His Kingdom must be your number one pursuit.

CHAPTER 4

LIFE IS MORE THAN THIS....

Therefore I say to you, do not worry about your life, what you will eat or what you will drink; nor about your body, what you will put on. Is not life more than food and the body more than clothing?

Matthew 6:25

Understanding the principles that govern life is absolutely essential in living a life of purpose. Previously, we established in clear terms the purpose of life and acknowledged the factors that could be real detractors in this journey, let's go a step further in understanding how life should be invested.

Any smart-thinking entrepreneur understands the value of making profits in business. No business exists just for the sake of being around. Besides the supply of goods and services, is also the need to make valuable profits. On the other hand, any business that keeps recording continuous losses is on its way to extinction. In the same, God who brought you into this world has made great investments in your life that is sure to birth profitable outcome. Your days on earth aren't designed for losses, but gains beneficial to your society and gener-

THE ESSENCE AND VALUE OF LIFE

ation. You're here to be a plus, not a minus, and you have all it takes.

Due to ignorance of these facts, so many around the world trade wrongly in life, giving themselves in exchange for what leads to destruction. Millions are giving their lives in exchange for riches, wisdom and power. And on a daily basis, many more are being coerced or even induced to journey down this evil way that culminates in losses. Though these three inducements appear great enough to make a person devote his entire life but the Creator of life says it's foolishness. God who is the Source of life says: "Is not life more than this...."

Thus, in a lay man's term, if we place you on a weight balance and the opposite side place wisdom, riches, power, and all that can be desired, Jesus says that your life is more than them! In other words, your value outweighs all the things that money can buy; your worth is superior to all things you get anxious and uptight about. Therefore it would be a terrible error to give yourself in exchange for these three things. Is not life more...!

You are more than these. The life in you is superlative in value; incomparable in worth, greater in essence. Is not life more.... What you have is more than what you need, and what you have will surely make a way for you.

Those who trade their lives for these allurements we mentioned are doing bad business, and are on their way to experiencing losses and extinction of purpose. It's an absolute abuse to give your life in exchange for money. I know it's very typical in our African Continent, where people sacrifice innocent lives in ritualistic killing in exchange for wealth. It's just like exchanging a Billion US dollar for a lead pencil. Value is not in things primarily, value is in lives.

This is best explicable when we see European countries and many developed nations that have very little or no natural resource yet are the economic powers of the world today with staggering GDP values. Yet African countries full of natural resources such as diamonds, gold, crude oil, cocoa, timber etc suffering in abject poverty and penury simply because their understanding of value is wrong. They think those minerals are their greatest resource, not knowing that the greatest resource on earth is the human life.

This is what the richest and most advanced nations practice: investing in their human resources, valuing the human life and making solid investments in the minds of their citizens, and in return enjoying enormous profit from the use of their potentials in nation building. Is not life more....!

THE SUPERIORITY OF LIFE

Behold, I give you the authority to trample on serpents and scorpions, and over all the power of the enemy, and nothing shall by any means hurt you. Nevertheless do not rejoice in this, that the spirits are subject to you, but rather rejoice because your names are written in heaven.

Luke 10:19-20

What get's you excited the most or what you love to boast about is a vivid reflection of your true character and priority. This passage of scripture bears a similar tone with the key scripture we have been analyzing. Jesus had bestowed His authority to His disciples to exercise power over satan and any evil force that would resist the advancement of the Kingdom, as He sent them out to preach the gospel. Thus, they were charged or equipped with mighty strength and wonder working abilities. But interestingly, the Lord added a most remarkable statement, saying that they weren't supposed to boast or rejoice about the fact that the spirits were subject to them; they weren't supposed to boast or get excited at how much power they had in their possession or offices they were occupying, but that their names were written in heaven, in the Book of Life.

This truth is so vital to reckon with because it reveals the nature of God, His reasoning and mind, and as well indicates how He expects us to see life. Jesus emphatically told his disciples not to rejoice about the fact that they were wielding tremendous value of strength, but in the fact that their names were registered in Heaven. In other words, the real value of life isn't in the transient authority or power we've been entrusted with. The real value of life is in your relationship with God. The life of God in you is superior to these fading glories, so, let God be your greatest value.

We need to live our lives from an eternal perspective by adopting God's viewpoint. Seeing things the way He sees them positions you to live life to its fullest. His perspective is that the life He's given you is of superlative value and mustn't be erroneously exchanged for power, wisdom or riches. The life in you is greater.

Just because you don't have all the good things of life today doesn't bring low your potential and value. Your value is not based on things; it stems from a relationship with the son of God. Your value isn't based on the type of make-up or shoes you wear, neither is it based on the office you work. Your value shouldn't be based on the fact that you're a consultant or own a lot of money. Neither should it be based on your country of residence or citizenship. That's not where true value lies. Your true value lies in exercising a real relationship with God who made you, and bringing the values of His kingdom to bear upon the heart of men in the world. Life is superior to the things we throw our weight on. What many regard as something, most at times is nothing, but vanity. For example the famous king Solomon who the wisest, richest and most powerful king acclaimed all these is vanity upon vanity. What carries weight is the value you place on your life and the lives of others. When you value yourself, you will value the people God surrounds you with. You will see beyond their failures, and value the treasures of life in them, whether they've been to school or not. Their skin colour makes no difference, every soul weighs the same value in God's sight, so, see the value in them.

Don't base your self-esteem on the wrong foundation such as college degrees, institutions you attended, the house you live, the exotic car you drive, the expensive dresses you have, the people you know, etc. Because when these things aren't available, your attitude and self-esteem in life would plunge! Besides God has warned us not to make these our boast, but rather boast in the relationship we have with Him.

There are individuals who stopped attending Church services because their dresses weren't as good as what some others wore in their assemblies, and in other not to look inferior to them refused to go for the meetings. In other words, they were giving up their access to the knowledge of life due to the transient absence of mere clothing. They have narrowed the whole concept of life to materials. Some even live life to appear big in terms of materials, wealth and class in front of their peers. That is very unnecessary and a big distraction to life itself.

"Is not life more than food and the body more than clothing?"

Understanding what matters the most puts you on the right track in the journey of life to make the right transactions that produce endless profits. The life in you is greater and superior to wisdom, power and riches. Value the precious gift of life!

What Makes or Mars Life

And you shall know the truth, and the truth shall make you free.

John 8:32

It's pretty easy to hear preachers talk about deliverance from demons or generational curses these days, but I strongly believe that a far greater and superior deliverance many need in our generation is coming to the knowledge of the truth about life, knowing what life is all about and how to make the best of one's days on earth.

It is not knowledge disclosed that makes men free, but knowledge applied. Knowledge when applied makes men free indeed. How much freedom you'd enjoy in your journey of life is up to you. When you decide to embrace the knowledge of the truth, your freedom or "deliverance" steps up to a higher level. You'd become free from the fears or life and deadly traps on the pathway.

By freedom here I refer to being unencumbered or breaking free from self-limiting thoughts and the passion to devote ones' life to the seductive force of wealth, wisdom and power.

Life really is a product of the choices we make. If your present situation is undesirable, you might be responsible. If you desire a change, you are equally responsible for effecting the transformation you desire.

Though you possess the responsibility of choosing the kind of life you desire, the quality of decisions you'd make would be based on the quality of information you receive and process. Right information positions you to make right decisions and moves, while the wrong information is more detrimental than you can imagine. Like some say, which I agree, you need to be rightly informed, so you don't end up deformed.

Your decisions can either make or mar your life. When a person sacrifices his life in exchange for power, wisdom or money, he's not only making an unprofitable transaction; but he's as well destroying the value of his own life. To devote yourself to these allurements of life is tantamount to undervaluing your life.

Do you recall the story of King Solomon who at the initial phase of his life had his priorities set right, and pursued the understanding of God for the singular purpose of fulfilling his assignment in life? Well, later on, he changed course and drifted away from the Kingdom, chasing after many strange women who gradually lured his heart away from God and values he once upheld. He became devoted to the worship of the pagan gods his numerous wives introduced him to and built shrines for them. This terrible diversion from the knowledge of the truth eventually cost him a loss of nearly his entire kingdom. But beyond this, his wisdom lost soundness and value.

In his own words, he said:

I, the Preacher, was king over Israel in Jerusalem. And I set my heart to seek and search out by wisdom concerning all that is done under heaven; this burdensome task God has given to the sons of man, by which they may be exercised. I have seen all the works that are done under the sun; and indeed, all is vanity and grasping for the wind. What is crooked cannot be made straight, And what is lacking cannot be numbered. I communed with my heart, saying. 'Look I have attained greatness, and have gained more wisdom than all who were before me in Jerusalem. My heart has understood great wisdom and knowledge. And I set my heart to know wisdom and to know madness and folly, I perceived that this also is grasping for the wind. For in much wisdom is much grief, And he who increases knowledge increases sorrow.

Ecclesiastes 1:12-18

The pursuit of wisdom wasn't his primary goal in life at the beginning, but when he failed and turned away from the Lord that became his pursuit and boasting, as well as his painful dissatisfaction, to the extent he said that in much wisdom is grief and he who increases knowledge increases sorrow.

At this point, his wisdom failed him, power brought him sorrows and wealth could not satisfy anymore, because the foundations were destroyed. He had marred the foundations of his life by making wrong choices:

King Solomon, however loved many foreign women besides Pharaoh's daughter-- Moabites, Ammonites, Edomites, Zidonians, and Hittites. They were from nations about which the Lord had told the Israelites, "You shall not intermarry with them because they will surely turn your hearts after their gods." Nevertheless, Solomon held fast to them in love.

1 Kings 11:1-2

When Solomon replaced his love for the Lord with love for foreign women, his kingdom values and pursuits became minified. He lost the passion for life, and began to consider everything about life as being meaningless and vanity. Nothing seemed valuable anymore, because life is all about God. When he fell in love with the very thing God warned him to flee from, failure was inevitable.

Falling in love with distractions of life is just like getting yourself trapped in bait. When you get hooked up in the wrong pursuit, you move away from the true path of life and embark on a mission that isn't designed to bring you fulfillment.

When you turn aside from God, you disconnect yourself from the very Essence of Life. When you ignore His values, you destroy the foundations of your being, and if your foundations are out of place, nothing you build will last for long: be it your family, finances or career, it will all come crashing down one day, because the substructure is out of place.

This explains why God took the kingdom away from Solomon, leaving him only with two tribes and giving out ten tribes to Jeroboam, because he had defied the Lord and ignored the values of the Kingdom. No distraction is worth the value of your life.

Then he said to Jeroboam, "Take ten pieces for yourself, for this is what the Lord, the God of Israel, says: 'See, I am going to tear the kingdom out of Solomon's hand and give you ten tribes.

---

1 Kings 11:31

Don't mar your life; neither destroy the value and essence of your being, because the consequences are extremely grievous. Let your values revolve around God and his principles for living, then and only then is foundation secure for generations to come. Build on a lasting legacy.

WORRY: A DISTRACTION OF PURPOSE

Doubtlessly, I would say that worry is a real distraction of a purpose-driven life. Not only is it detrimental to our health, but it has a way of turning our attention away from the real purpose of life: which is spreading the Kingdom of God on the face of the earth.

Jesus the Author of life said of Himself: "I am the Way, the Truth and the Life." In other words, He is the very Essence of life. His presence radiates and imparts life to all who draw near to Him. And most certainly, He knows a lot more about life than any person who ever lived. If He has something to say about life, the least we can do is listen and heed. One of the precautions He expressly gave concerning what to avoid in life is worry:

Therefore I say to you, do not worry about your life, what you will eat or what you will drink; nor about your body, what you will put on. Is not life more than food and the body more than clothing? Look at the birds of the air, for they neither sow nor reap nor gather into barns; yet your heavenly Father feeds them. Are you not of more value than they? Which of you by worrying can add one cubit to his stature? So why do you worry about clothing? Consider the lilies of the field, how they grow: they neither toil nor spin; and yet I say to you that even Solomon in all his glory was not arrayed like one of these. Now if God so clothes the grass of the field, which today is, and tomorrow is thrown into the oven, will He not much more clothe you, O you of little faith? Therefore do not worry, saying, 'What shall we eat?' or 'What shall we drink?' or 'What shall we wear? For after all these

things the Gentiles seek. For your heavenly Father knows that you need all these things. But seek first the kingdom of God and His righteousness, and all these things shall be added to you. Therefore do not worry about tomorrow, for tomorrow will worry about its own things. Sufficient for the day is its own trouble.

Matthew 6:25-34

Our human mind has a tendency to seek for solutions in the midst of every challenge. It works like a computer, scanning what possibly could be done to succour an impending need or deal with an anticipated challenge. Problems and needs are bound to come in life. We all face hardships, and deal with the storm clouds of adversity. Rather than be tossed to and fro in the whirlwind of anxious and worrisome thoughts when the storms of life rage around you, you can do something different and better: refuse to worry! Worry is a very serious and deadly distraction from the purpose of life.

Worry is an abuse of life. Don't worry about tomorrow, for tomorrow will worry about itself. Don't worry about how your needs will be met, rather, use your mind to create solutions for your life. Worry takes you from somewhere to nowhere and depletes your strength. The moment you kick-start on worry, your mind loses its ability to create solutions or receive ideas, and as result your pains are magnified than minified.

The problems of life shouldn't derail your purpose or divert your focus. They shouldn't get you stuck in the chains of worry and fear. In fact it's an abuse of life when we get ourselves in bouts of worry, as it diminishes our focus on the essence and value of life. Not only worry, but attitudes such as inferiority complex, pride and fear are equally harmful and can mar the very essence of your being. These all can lead to depression, stress, fatigue and other health disorders that would surely hamper your effectiveness and well being in life.

But when you take the right approach of seeking first the Kingdom of God and His righteousness, by engaging the entirety of your being in pursuing the knowledge of God and the spreading of His values such as kindness, justice, and righteousness on earth, your needs would gravitate towards their solution and things would fall in place for you. When you pursue the greater purpose of life: the Kingdom, the lesser things of life will automatically flow towards you.

I love to describe this scripture of Matthew 6:33 as the law of additional blessings: *"But seek first the kingdom of God and His righteousness, and all these things shall be added to you."*

All these things others worry about will be added when you make the kingdom your pursuit in life. Even personal needs, desires and wants will eventually be met; they will be added unto you when the Kingdom becomes your priority.

MAKING PROFITS IN THE BUSINESS OF LIFE

Thus says the LORD, your Redeemer, The Holy One of Israel: "I am the LORD your God, Who teaches you to profit, Who leads you by the way you should go.

Isaiah 48:17

God desires that you live a profitable and fruitful life. If you embrace Kingdom principles and exalt these values in your human endeavours, you'd be sure to make profits in life.

Profit making is vital for the success of any business endeavour. Besides meeting genuine needs and solving relevant problems comes the undeniable need of being lucrative in one's venture. Life is a business that necessitates profit making. In one of his parables, Jesus described a certain servant as being unprofitable and wasteful with life (Matt. 25:30).

In other words, his efforts or lack of it engendered losses for both himself and his master. God who gave you the gift of life desires to see tangible gains or positive outputs from your endeavours.

In life there will come opportunities at certain times. Your ability to recognize them, cease them and translate them into results in line with your essence for being alive is what we term as being profitable. It's important to note that not every opportunity repeats itself; thus, you need to be well prepared to cease every God-given opportunity that comes your way and make the most of them.

For what is a man profited, if he shall gain the whole world, and lose his own soul? Or what will a man give in exchange for his soul?

Matthew 16:26

To trade your life in exchange for riches, power or wisdom is an unwise investment that's sure to result in loss. Life is more important than wisdom. Life is superior to power. Life is greater than wealth.

The value of your soul is greater than all the wealth and riches that could be found on earth. Your soul is of superior worth to all the diamonds, gold and precious stones on this planet. No amount of money is worth giving in exchange for your soul.

Besides, your life is of superior value to wisdom. No amount of wisdom or philosophy is greater than the essence of your being. To give your soul in exchange for this is sure to result in loss. Something of a higher value should not be exchanged for something of a lower value. If you take a million dollars and use it to pay for one bottle of coca cola, you would be viewed as insane. With that amount of money, you could build your own factory for producing coca cola. It is too disproportional. That is what we do when we give our lives in exchange for any or all of these three allurements of life.

Moreover, no amount of fame, power or influence is greater than the value of a man's life. No political office or ambition is worth destroying one's life or endangering other lives for. To give your life in exchange for power would eventually end in loss, because you're worth more than these.

Moreover, any gains that emerge from wisdom, power or riches are transient and temporary. The greatest and most valuable essence to give your life for is the kingdom. Seeking first the Kingdom!

The Kingdom of God is the only concern worth giving our lives in exchange for. In fact, the most profitable transaction one could ever make is to give one's life for the kingdom. God's kingdom is the singular and greatest.

GOLDEN NUGGETS

1. What you have is more than what you need, and what you have will surely make a way for you.

2. Real value of life is not in the transient authority or power we have been entrusted with, but in our relationship with God.

3. It is knowledge applied, not knowledge disclosed that makes men free.

4. Our human mind has a tendency to seek solutions in the midst of every challenge.

5. Worry takes you from somewhere to nowhere and depletes your strength.

6. God who gave you the gift of life desires to see tangible gains or positive outputs from your endeavours.

7. Life's most persistent and urgent question is "what are you doing for others?'

CHAPTER 5

THE VALUABLE DEVOTION OF LIFE

Great peace have those who love your law, and nothing causes them to stumble.

Psalm 119:165

Of what essence is there to life when there is no peace of mind and rest? A troubled and depressed mind is a burden to endure, especially when purpose for living is unknown. The problem of depression has inadvertently culminated in a global rise of suicidal rates, thus, becoming a source of major concern in our society, one we cannot ignore. Knowing how valuable life is, destroying oneself is a tragic loss that must be averted!

According to the World Health Organization: *"Every 40 seconds, one person commits suicide somewhere in the world, which tallies to 800,000 suicides annually, worldwide."*

In an article dated June 7th, 2015 by Fredric Neuman M.D. on "Fighting Fear", he categorically said:

"Many thousands of Americans kill themselves every year. It is said that for every successful suicide, there are ten men and women who attempt suicide. And for every one of those, there are ten who think of killing themselves, but do not. It is presumed that the underlying cause of such thoughts is depression; and that is usually the case."

With the recent economic recession in our country, Nigeria, there's also been a corresponding increase in suicidal cases. The despair and depression which has led many to take their lives has mainly been due to the financial strain and unemployment difficulties that's been so prevalent in recent times.

I was deeply touched when I heard the story of a 21-year old man, named Chinonso who committed suicide after drinking a substance suspected to be rat poison in Byazhin village, Kubwa; a satellite of the Federal Capital Territory, FCT. The deceased was said to have dropped a note for his mother that he wanted "to go and rest."

A recent report proved that 90% of people who commit suicide suffer from untreated depression. Implying that, nine out of every ten people who commit suicide do so because of the sad feelings, emotional dejections or discouragements they're struggling with.

I was so appalled when I heard the story of a 23-year old man, who committed suicide in FESTAC Town, Lagos, due to the stigmatization and rejection he faced by people because of his skin colour, being albino. Unfortunately, he resolved to end his reproach by taking his own life.

Life was never meant to be lived in fear and depression or end in suicide. Our lives thrive only in a conducive climate of peace. That tranquil state of the mind is an absolute necessity for fruitful living. You need great peace to discover, recover and fulfill your purpose in life.

Great peace have those who love your law, and nothing causes them to stumble.

Psalm 119:165

Great peace here refers to the overwhelming tranquillity, absolute calmness, and prosperity that exceed the worries, external issues or concerns of life that bombard our minds. It is a fact that we all are faced with various problems, ranging from the economic hardships in our nation, religious crises in our communities or personal issues or hurts in human relationships. These various factors are capable of contributing in one way or the other to depressive bouts if we hold on to them, thereby stealing away our peace and joy in life.

You need to be fully armed and loaded with great peace in order to live life to the fullest and maximize your purpose on earth. You may not be entirely responsible for what's happening around you, but you're responsible for what is happening inside of you. You're responsible for living a life of peace. Great peace belongs to those who love the law of God, and nothing can successful stop them in their journey of life.

Besides other meanings, to love means to be devoted, dedicated and committed wholly to a person or cause. Love is expressed through devotion. I can tell what you love by observing what you devote most of your leisure time to, because love is proven by devotion, and your devotion ultimately determines your peace.

Those who devote their lives to money, power or wisdom may never enjoy lasting peace. These factors on their own don't impart peace. A person who is broke and in huge debts might easily conclude that if he has a lot of money and clears off his debts, then he would be happy and successful. Unfortunately, it's not always the case. True and lasting happiness doesn't emanate from having a lot of money, or occupying a powerful position.

Neither does devoting one's self to the pursuit of wisdom bring about peace.

Peace flows from a living relationship with the person of Jesus Christ. Great peace belongs to those who devote themselves to knowing and applying the principles and laws of God. Those who commit themselves to understanding God and the Kingdom values of life as revealed in the scriptures, and make these the foundation of their lives are the ones who benefit from this great peace.

When you devote yourself to these enduring truths, you would never stumble or fail in life. Despite the alarming rate of evil occurrences, nothing you do would fail, because you're founded on the Author of life and steadfastly devoted to the values and principles of life, and thus well anchored to weather every storm.

I would like to emphasize that devoting oneself to wisdom, wealth or power won't produce peace. Peace comes from devoting yourself to the knowledge of God and the spread of His values on earth.

Great peace is enjoyed by those who love God's law; whose hearts pant to understand His principles for life and make every effort to live out those values. Peace is the necessary atmosphere for your success in life. When peace reigns within your heart, fear and anxiety find it hard to penetrate your mind. When peace pervades your inmost thoughts, depression can hardly penetrate your being.

You will keep him in perfect peace, Whose mind is stayed on You, Because he trusts in You.

Isaiah 26:3

What you devote your attention to will ultimately determine your peace. If you fix your mind on the allurements of life, your life would be devoid of peace, on the contrary, if you place your mind on God and His values of kindness, justice and righteousness, you'll experience a flood of boundless peace. You need to create this atmosphere of peace for your productivity in life by becoming addicted to God's Word. Embrace His perspectives and exalt His viewpoints above what is commonly celebrated. These days, the popular opinion and what sells best mostly contradict the lifestyle and values of the kingdom. But we must be smart to understand that these are paths to destruction, and not life.

Those who devote themselves to the pursuit of power, wisdom or riches will always struggle in life without peace. Because these factors aren't designed to be your main reason for living, but meant to facilitate your essence of living, they are tools to accomplish your purpose on earth; they shouldn't occupy the centre stage of your life.

The more you embrace and esteem God's understanding of life: His principles and values, nothing could cause you to stumble, because they become a guiding light on your journey to keeping you from error or falling prey to the enticing traps of life. When you fall in love with His ways of doing things and His perspectives on life, your journey in life takes on a transcendent dimension. You'd think differently, talk differently and act differently from the rest of the world. Your perspectives, views and attitude in life will be radically different from that of the average folk who isn't as informed as you. And as a result you will be a wonder to many.

Two Cardinal Perspectives of Life

For My thoughts are not your thoughts, Nor are your ways My ways, says the LORD. For as the heavens are higher than the earth, so are My ways higher than your ways, And My thoughts than your thoughts.

Isaiah 55:8-9

Life is really about choice-making, choosing rightly. Your outcome in life will be based on the choices you make. Where you are today maybe as a result of a series of choices you've made in the past; and where you'll be in the near future will also be the direct consequence of the next decisions. If you aren't pleased with the quality of life you've been living, you need to make re-adjustments. You need a transformation in the outlook of life and a corresponding change in your choices. You need to make better choices to move ahead in order to achieve your purpose on earth. That's really how to take charge of your life. Don't leave your life to chances, make the right decisions and take responsibility for your future.

You have the power of choice: to decide what perspective you'd live by and how your life would turn out. But the truth about our choices is that our decisions are mostly based on our perspectives or viewpoints; how we see life.

This reminds me of the twelve spies who were dispatched by Moses on espionage to the Promised Land. Their assignment was to spy the land, make certain vital observations and report to the leader after 40 days. On their return and report, ten out of the twelve spies made a report that it was impossible to enter the Promised Land while only two submitted that conquering the enemy land was an easy task to undertake owing to the advantage of God's presence. The Ten spies brought an evil report of unbelief of the land poisoning the minds of many others, while two brought a good report of the land, inspiring the faith of others in God to possess their inheritance. The ten had a completely different perspective of the land from the two; and their perspective influenced their choice of thoughts, words, actions, and eventual outcome - they never entered the Promised Land along with those who embraced their opinion. I would like to say at this point, be careful whose opinions you believe. Who you believe determines your future.

But the other two spies: Caleb and Joshua who saw from a higher perspective of faith in God, entered the Promised Land and conquered new terrains for the Kingdom. Indeed your perspective determines where you'd end in life. You don't have to embrace an opinion or viewpoint simply because it's popular or major. When it comes to a life of success and fulfillment, what wins at the end of the day isn't the majority or the popular opinion on polls, but the truth - God's perspective.

Therefore, I can boldly conclude that there are two main perspectives that frame the minds of many and influence the choices they make on a daily basis. There is God's perspective and Man's perspective to life, and these two viewpoints have astronomical differences.

God's perspective is His viewpoint on the essence of life: what He expects life to be for all His children, how

He wants us to live life, His outlook on life and what He desires us to emphasize in life.

It's a notable fact that what God places greater emphasis on in life differs significantly from what many do. Naturally speaking, His thoughts differ from our thoughts; His ways are usually diametrically opposed from our ways. The difference in fact is as high as the heavens are above the earth.

Thus, man's perspective on the other side is simply the viewpoints many embrace and choose to live their lives from.

Take for instance, there are folks who think that the reason they came into this world was to simply get educated, obtain a good paying job, get married and raise children and grandchildren if possible. And when their wards in whom they've made the most of their lives' investments fall short of their expectations or dreams, they begin to reconsider and question the main reason for their being alive.

The essence of life is way beyond child bearing and income-making. Life is more than gaining a degree and pursuing a career. Life is all about purpose. The true significance of life is seeing and living from the Creator's viewpoint. How He sees life really matters the most, not how we see it or popular opinions passed down to us.

According to the scriptures, the essence of life is really about purpose: discovering and fulfilling God's purpose or assignment for your being on earth. This is your Creator's perspective.

YOUR SET TIME HAS COME

You will arise and have mercy on Zion; For the time to favor her, Yes, the set time, has come.

Psalm 102:13

Have you ever wondered: "why am I alive on earth today? Why wasn't I born a century ago or in the future decades to come? It is because your set time has come. Your season is here.

Ecclesiastes 3:1-2 gives us a further clue:

"To everything there is a season, a time for every purpose under heaven: A time to be born, and a time to die; a time to plant, and a time to pluck what is planted."

You're alive on earth today because from God's perspective, your time has come. It's your season; that's the reason you're here now. You were fashioned by God for a season and a reason. You are born to solve a problem, meet a need, which may not have existed several years ago, or came into existence at the time of your birth.

You are here now because God needs you and the world needs you!

There is a season for everything and a time for every purpose under heaven. When it's season for orange fruits, it becomes a whole lot easy to find oranges in groceries and fruit stores. In the same way, you're here now because it's your time and season to answer to the need for which you were born.

"GIVE ME A PLACE TO STAND ON, AND I
WILL MOVE THE EARTH."

ARCHIMEDES

Get rid of distractions, have the right focus. Then, indeed you will move the earth like Archimedes said. The time has come for you to rise up and meet those needs for which the Creator has ordained for you to solve. You are a savior from Mount Zion, sent of God to accomplish a certain task and bring succor to the pains of humanity. Now your job is to find out what your task is and get busy fulfilling it. You have no business spending all your life on something that isn't related to your life's purpose. No matter what endeavors of life may be your present preoccupation that differs entirely from your ultimate assignment, you must still create quality space and time in the present for your unique assignment: time to develop yourself for the task so that your purpose will not be lost. This is the primary purpose of your life.

Mordecai in scriptures, who was known as Esther's cousin and adoptive father boldly declared to Queen Esther when Haman the king's favorite threatened to annihilate all the Jews:

For if you remain completely silent at this time, relief and deliverance will arise for the Jews from another place, but you and your father's house will perish. Yet who knows whether you have come to the kingdom for such a time as this?

Esther 4:14

Where do you stand in the spread of the kingdom in your country?

Are you simply an onlooker praying that one day the Almighty God will visit your country and save your land from all the corrupt practices, economic hardships and the uncountable vices destroying innocent lives in your time?

Or are you like Mordecai, Esther and other dedicated Jews who vowed to lay down their lives to save their nation? Before embarking on her risky mission to oppose and avert the impending destruction that was to be executed by the enemies of her nation, Esther said: "If I perish, I perish." The Queen wasn't afraid to die for her nation.

> "IF A MAN HASN'T DISCOVERED SOMETHING THAT HE WILL DIE FOR, HE ISN'T FIT TO LIVE."

Life is a risk, and until you discover what you're willing to die for, you haven't discovered what you're willing to live for.

Esther never died on this mission, because those who lay down their lives for the Kingdom always have it restored. She saved her nation, saved a posterity and passed on a kingdom legacy for the unborn generations. She was a savior from Mount Zion.

Whenever I cogitate on this scripture, I feel the humongous sense of responsibility I owe to my generation to bring the kingdom to their reach, to make the values and principles of our kingdom a tangible reality that no man can deny.

The need for the Kingdom is so germane especially in my own nation and land of birth, Nigeria. I was born for such a time as this; I have come for such a season as this. I thank God for His special grace upon my life to bring to light the Gospel of His Kingdom to Ukraine and many nations of the former soviet nations, Europe as well as the Middle East. But now, I have a burning desire in my heart to see God's kingdom take roots in every sphere of human endeavors in my beloved nation. I can boldly testify that I have come into the kingdom for such a time as this.

I want you to know as you read through the lines of this book, that this is your set time to bring God's kingdom to your nation. This is your season to superimpose the values of the kingdom in your world on a daily basis. Your kingdom purpose preceded your birth. You are here because your time has come, and you must make a difference. You can't afford to seat on the fence and keep on registering your complaints. God didn't bring you into this world to be a spectator or complainer; you are here to make a difference that cannot be denied. You are here to bring about societal transformations in line with the lifestyle of the kingdom. Taking the sideline or doing nothing is akin to refusing to fulfill the reason for your being. You need to rise up and take charge.

I'm definitely not referring to joining a service unit in your Church and cleaning up the pews. That's good but too preliminary. I'm referring to purposefully living out the values of kindness, righteousness and justice in your day to day affairs. I'm talking about exalting the virtues of love, mercy, honesty, integrity, sincerity and imparting the principles of the kingdom in your workplace or sphere of calling.

Where others cheat, you practice truth and verity. Where others steal, you uphold honesty and accountability. Where injustice reigns, you bring in mercy and justice, upholding the truth above the fear of man. I'm talking about a kingdom invasion in our world, not religion. Jesus came to bring the Kingdom, not religion. He was killed by religious sects, but raised to life by the power of the living God, because He laid down His life to bring the kingdom of God to our hearts and our world.

The Kingdom purpose for your existence is incomparably greater than the needs of religion. We have so much of religion and so little of kingdom values. Every child of God has a significant role to play in the kingdom. Your place in the kingdom is non-negotiable. Therefore, don't devote your life to the wrong stuffs; the kingdom is what matters, it is what will count for eternity. The kingdom is your reason for living.

Never think the government, pastors or some selected folks are the ones to cause the changes we want to see. You are the one to impact your world. You are the one to live for others. You are the one to give love, life, hope and faith to your generation. What is that thing you have a passion for that will speak compassion to your world? Go ahead and start doing something. Don't wait for a seemingly perfect timing. It never comes, start with what you have. You have what it takes to make a change.

THE MOST VALUABLE DEVOTION OF LIFE

"But seek first the kingdom of God and His righteousness, and all these things shall be added to you."

Matthew 6:33

Make the Kingdom of God your most valuable devotion in life. Make it your greatest passion to understand the kingdom of God and how to bring its influence to bear upon your society. The whole world is waiting for the manifestations of the sons of God, the mature sons who have the training and understanding of the kingdom. The purpose of joining a local assembly is to receive training on how to bring the kingdom into your sphere of contact, because this is the main purpose of life.

When young recruits join the army, they receive serious training on how to defend their nations even before such a need is at hand. Every responsible nation has its Defense academy or military institution responsible for recruiting, raising and sending well disciplined soldiers to defend the cause of the nation: men who would gladly die for an earthly nation or kingdom. In the same way, you should or have joined a local church not to become a benchwarmer or church worker, but to get spiritually trained and sent forth with the sole mission of spreading the kingdom in your world. Just like salt does no good by remaining locked inside the salt-shaker, a believer will do no good by restraining himself from positively influencing his society. You are a kingdom agent of national transformation. You have the Bible and the Holy Spirit to guide you on how to introduce the values and principles of the kingdom to the needs of people in your world. The needs of people are your primary opportunities; their problems are your access points; their pains are your platforms for change. The kingdom thrives the most in areas of pain and desperate needs. If you look through scriptures, you'd see that before Jesus performed a miracle there was first an obvious need of humanity, and He always took advantage of that need to introduce the principles of the Kingdom, because the kingdom is like a bright light that shines in the midst of the darkness.

Dear friend, we hail from this same heavenly Kingdom that knows no end; an eternal kingdom superior to all kingdoms of men. We have Jesus Christ as our King of kings, Author of life and Captain of our salvation: who first loved us and laid down His dear life for ours. He has recruited you into His army so you can take His salvation to the unsaved and introduce His kingdom into your nation. And He has promised to be with you as we undertake the assignment of kingdom expansion till the very end of time.

> "WHEN YOU DISCOVER YOUR MISSION YOU WILL FEEL ITS DEMAND. IT WILL FILL YOU WITH ENTHUSIASM AND A BURNING DESIRE TO GET TO WORK ON IT."
>
> W. CLEMENT STONE

Our kingdom unlike the kingdom of men is one with eternal rewards. Our sacrifices and devotions will receive everlasting rewards and honor. The best investments in life are those that enhance kingdom spread and expansion.

Hence, the kingdom should be the most valuable devotion in life. Invest your life, energy, time and resources there and give it your utmost priority.

Remember, time is life. Therefore, don't live the rest of yours in pursuit of riches. Neither should you give your life in exchange for power or wisdom. These factors like we earlier emphasized aren't bad, but must be seen in the right perspective, as tools designed for the fulfillment of our Kingdom purpose. This is the sole essence of life!

THE MISSING DAY FOUND

As we bring this chapter to a close, I strongly wish to stir your undiluted mind towards a wholesome pursuit of the knowledge and understanding of God and spread of His kingdom above all else.

The value of all knowledge and learning; be it scientific, philosophical, or arts all find their true value and relevance in the knowledge of God, and without this foundation it is of no value to life. To devote oneself to any learning that contradicts the knowledge of God and values of the kingdom is most detrimental and sure to lead one away from the very essence of life. Life ought to be lived from understanding and perspective of God.

When Moses prayed that God would: *"Teach us to number our days that we may apply our hearts to wisdom"* it was obvious from his knowledgeable request that the time-factor is so significant to life, in fact time is life. When a man's time is up, he's gone! Thus the value of one day is so vital in the fulfillment of purpose. Every day is important and we must make it count. The older folks tend to value every day and treasure every waking moment of life than the younger, because they've understood the value of time. Therefore, we must devote everyday judiciously towards realizing the essence of being alive. Every moment, day, hour, minute and even second must be conscientiously invested in the pursuit of purpose.

Do you remember the story in the Bible of when the Sun stood still in the book of Joshua as the Israelites battled against the Gibeonites (Joshua 10:13)? Some years back, the U.S. National Aeronautics and Space Administration (NASA) made an astounding discovery in this area that underscored this Bible truth. A man named Harold Hill, a NASA consultant and president of Curtis Engine Company, described how NASA computers were looking back in time when they issued an alert that something was wrong. There seemed to be a missing day from the calculations. The scientists puzzled over this a long time until someone in their midst reflected that in the Bible, there's a story about the day the Sun stood still for the Hebrew leader Joshua. This almost solved the puzzle. According to the computer calculations, not an entire day was lost, but 23 hours and 20 minutes. But there was a new problem. What about the other 40 minutes? That's when the same employee remembered that there's another story in the Bible about a day when the sun moved backwards 10 degrees which is an arc of 40 minutes in the era of King Hezekiah (2 Kings 20:9-11). Thus the entire question of the missing day is solved!

Well, what's the main lesson here? Each day you have on earth is an opportunity or a divine entrustment of time by your Creator to fulfill your purpose. You need to purposefully devote each day to the pursuit and spread of His Kingdom.

But, beloved, be not ignorant of this one thing, that one day is with the Lord as a thousand years, and a thousand years as one day.

2 Peter 3:8

A day with the Lord is like a thousand years, and a thousand years is like one day. In other words, any day you spend in God's presence and for His kingdom has the value of a thousand years impact. Can you imagine that? A day with Jesus is like a thousand years. The best way then to spend time is with the Lord. Investing time in fellowship with the Lord and fulfilment of His kingdom purpose on earth would automatically multiply the value of your time a thousand times more. This is one of the reasons I take out time for personal retreats and early morning devotions, because when I begin my day in His presence, spending time in His Word and prayer, not only do I enjoy the moments, but I receive inspirations that would transform my life and position me to bring about lasting changes in the society and other nations. A day with Him is like a thousand years. On the other hand, a thousand years without Him is like a day. That is, it doesn't matter how long you live, but how well. Even if you are given a thousand years to live on earth, as a believer in Jesus; without a devotion to the kingdom and His purpose for your life on earth, it would amount to nothing but waste of time.

Therefore, every day is absolutely important. Every day is another opportunity to live life to the fullest, so maximize the moments of your life purposefully. Everyday counts, so make it count.

GOLDEN NUGGETS

1. Our lives thrive only in a conducive climate of peace – a tranquil state of our mind.

2. You need to be fully armed and loaded with great peace in order to live life to the fullest and maximize your purpose on earth.

3. I can tell what you love by observing what you devote most of your time to because love is proven by devotion.

4. There are two main perspectives to life – The God's perspective and man's perspective. God's perspective is what He expects life to be for all His children.

5. Life is a risk and until you discover what you are willing to die for, you haven't discovered what you are willing to live for.

6. You are here to bring about societal transformations in line with the lifestyle of the kingdom.

7. Every moment, day, hour, minute and even second must be conscientiously invested in the pursuit of purpose.

PART 2

HOW TO TRULY LIVE

CHAPTER 6

LIVING FROM GOD'S PERSPECTIVE

"ANYONE WHO STOPS LEARNING IS OLD, WHETHER THIS HAPPENS AT 20 OR 80. ANYONE WHO KEEPS ON LEARNING NOT ONLY REMAINS YOUNG, BUT BECOMES CONSISTENTLY MORE VALUABLE REGARD-LESS OF PHYSICAL CAPACITY."

HARVEY ULLMAN

Life is a journey of learning; learning how to live. Being alive comes along with the life-long responsibility of learning and self-education, because the moment you stop learning, you start dying! The moment you stop learning, you become irrelevant to your world. Growth ends where learning ceases.

Have you ever noticed there are folks you know who are literally at the same spot today as they were seven years ago? They still have the same dreams, the same problems, the same alibis, the same opportunities, the same way of thinking, and the same old perspective. They aren't advancing in life.

It's appears as if they unplugged their clocks at a certain point in life in time and stayed at a fixed moment. However, God's will for us is to grow, to continue to learn and improve. The biggest room in our house is always the room for self-improvement.

"EVERYBODY WANTS TO BE: NOBODY
WANTS TO GROW."

GOETHE

An important way to keep growing is to never stop asking questions. The person who is afraid of asking is ashamed of learning. Life's most important answers can be found in asking the right questions. We should learn as if we will live forever and live as if we will die tomorrow.

"TODAY A READER. TOMORROW A LEADER."

W. FUSSELMAN

Remember life is in seasons, just like we have winter, summer, spring and autumn. Every season is special and requires you to make certain adjustments. For instance when it's the rainy season, you might need to take umbrellas along with you, as such adjustments might be necessary. Learning or being a learner helps you to always make the appropriate adjustments to thrive in all seasons of life. You can't say, "I've always known this and I'm going to stick with the past." No! In life, you learn and grow; and you grow to take up responsibilities.

This cycle of life, places on you the humbling task of being a lifelong student in the path of life, because when you're faced with new challenges in the fulfillment of your purpose, you need fresh understanding of God's perspective to make the needed difference. So, your process of learning continues.

You may graduate from a University or Polytechnic, but you don't graduate from the University of Life. For as long as you live, your classes remain valid. Therefore, open your mind to the art of self-education. Develop a lifelong habit of studying, and learning.

LIVING TO LEARN

Every time I think about my country, I think about responsibility, what I must do to save my nation, because learning and growing places a tremendous sense of responsibility on me. Before God and man, I must make a difference. I strongly believe that life is all about making a difference; birthing transformations that result in the spread of the Kingdom on earth. We are wired to carry the values and virtues of the Kingdom into every sphere of our human society. That's a reason you must keep on learning and growing.

When Moses talks about life, he says prayerfully to God: *"Teach us to number our days that we may apply our hearts to understanding."* The very first words he mentions in this particular reference to the essence and value of life is "Teach us." Meaning you need to be taught about life; you have to make great efforts to comprehend the essence and value of life, in order not abuse the purpose of your existence. Everyone has a purpose to play in life; every individual has a role to fulfill on earth, but when we fail to conscientiously apply our hearts to the understanding of how life should be lived, we could end up not fulfilling the very reason for which we were brought to this world. You need to get well versed on the essence and value of life.

Unfortunately, there are no curriculums or courses in our Schools, Colleges or Universities on the subject of life, though we've invested a lot of finances there. Even some in spiritual leadership lack accurate understanding and training on this most vital subject of life. But thank God for the Bible. It has a lot to say about life. It is extremely rich on this subject and contains accurate answers of our Creator's perspective on how life must be lived.

Little wonder Paul instructed his protégé, Timothy:

Study to shew thyself approved unto God, a workman that needeth not to be ashamed, rightly dividing the word of truth.

2 Timothy 2:15 KJV

Studying and learning brings approval in life, and to truly live from God's perspective, you must humble yourself and become a learner for life. Paul himself was a diligent student of life. So serious was his commitment that when he invited Timothy to come for a visit, he specifically requested that he came along with his books and parchments:

"Bring the cloak that I left with Carpus at Troas when you come – and the books, especially the parchments."

2 Timothy 4:13

While some are busy spending a lot of their hard-earned income on makeup, nice dresses, shoes and brand new cars, you should be investing more on your mind, invest more into books and training programs. Take up a new course and improve your skills. Improve yourself and enlarge your capacity through knowledge. When you become a committed learner in life, then you'd surely make a difference in life.

Jesus said in the scriptures that after accepting Him as Saviour, the very next thing is to begin learning:

Come to Me, all you who labor and are heavy laden, and I will give you rest. Take My yoke upon you and learn from Me, for I am gentle and lowly in heart, and you will find rest for your souls.

Matthew 11:28-29

After being born again, some believers just loaf around waiting for the Rapture to suddenly occur, oblivious of these crucial words of Jesus: *"Take my yoke upon you and learn from me..."* You're to begin learning about Jesus and His principles for life. You're to become a diligent learner if you're going to succeed in live. Success in life is never accidental, it comes through learning.

If you're worn out or tired about life; if your journey has been one of immense disappointments, discouragements, despairs and heartaches, I strongly recommend you come to Jesus and surrender completely to Him. Ask Him to become your Saviour and Lord, and allow His peace to flood your soul. When He steps into the quarters of your heart, your life will be renewed and your strength restored. He will remove your heavy burden and give a light yoke - the yoke of learning from Him. Do this now.

Learning is the yoke you're to bear in life. It's a light burden that brings rest and ease to your soul. Those who commit to learning and improving themselves will make fewer mistakes in the journey of life than those who simply go through the motions, because life is all about learning.

LEARNING IS A MOST INTEGRAL ASPECT OF LIVING.

Learning is a most integral aspect of living. Without learning you cannot truly live. Without learning from God's Word, you can't live successfully from His perspective. So devote yourself to learning in your journey of life.

When people are a little bit exposed in life, they become too proud to learn new things. Be humble to learn, unlearn and relearn. Unlearn the wrong information you have received and mind set you had created in the past. Replace them with the right ones. When a better revelation comes to you, don't be afraid to improve on the old. Don't stay glued to those gabbages you have received which can't take you anywhere. Be ready to re learn. Be an ardent learner.

LIVING BY HIS TRADEMARKS

"GOD'S Message: Don't let the wise brag of their wisdom. Don't let heroes brag of their exploits. Don't let the rich brag of their riches. If you brag, brag of this and this only: That you understand and know me. I'm GOD, and I act in loyal love. I do what is right and set things right and fair, and delight in those who do the same things. These are my trademarks."

Jeremiah 9:23-24 (Message Translation)

To live from God's perspective and see life from His angle, you need to gain valuable insight on what He detests and delights in life. You need to comprehend His trademarks. Our verses of scripture enlighten us on this.

During the early years of our marriage, my most passionate desire besides understanding God's plan for marriage was to know my beautiful Princess, Pastor Bose, whom the Lord has given me for a wife. I wanted to know what she liked or loved and what she detested or disliked. Though several years have gone-by, I can honestly say, I'm still learning. Today, the common understanding and perspective we share in life have gone a long way in deepening our relationship and prospering our home.

When two separate individuals come together and embrace the same perspective, ideologies and mindset towards life, journeying together becomes a whole lot easier and exciting, because their focus is unified.

Can two walk together, unless they are agreed?

Amos 3:3

You don't have to live a thousand years to comprehend all the intricacies and bewildering mysteries about life. All you have to do is to become a learner; learning from the One who's lived way longer than anyone ever did. He is God the creator. The oldest person hasn't lived up to a day to God. He pre-existed you: He is the One who knows the beginning and end of time. In fact He created time and life; and He is Life. He is so much more than we can say. Thus, the wisest decision you could ever make is to adopt His understanding; embrace His mindset and come to terms with His outlook on life: knowing what He loves and what He detests, and making these the guiding light of your life.

The Message translation is blunt and clear in the expression of this truth regarding God's outlook on life. First He shows us what mustn't brag or pride ourselves about. God dislikes it when we brag about our wisdom: what we've known and practiced. That's why the scripture says:

Let another man praise you, and not your own mouth; a stranger, and not your own lips.

Proverbs 27:2

Praising yourself and bragging about your wisdom, exploits or riches is a very unwise thing. The error in so doing is that we fail to give credit to those through whom we acquired such wisdom; others who helped us on journey to success and most of all, our Creator who granted us access to these treasures of life as well as the very gift of life.

Everything you have is a gift. Your wisdom: what you know; your exploits: what you've accomplished; your wealth: what you possess were all given to you by God. If these all are gifts, why brag about them and make them the central focus of your existence? What do you have that you weren't given?

For who makes you differ from another? And what do you have that you did not receive? Now if you did indeed receive it, why do you boast as if you had not received it?

1 Corinthians 4:7

When you live with this understanding of life as a gift, there would be no room for unnecessary boasting or showing off, because you know that all you have is a gift: the wisdom, power and riches are all gifts in life, so there's no need to pat yourself on the back: saying "I did this or that all by myself." The moment Nebuchadnezzar, the King of Babylon began doing this and was carried away by how great he thought he was, immediately he was deposed of his kingdom and humbled by God:

The king spoke, saying, "Is not this great Babylon, that I have built for a royal dwelling by my mighty power and for the honor of my majesty? While the word was still in the king's mouth, a voice fell from heaven: King Nebuchadnezzar, to you it is spoken: the kingdom has departed from you! And they shall drive you from men, and your dwelling shall be with the beasts of the field. They shall make you eat grass like oxen; and seven times shall pass over you, until you know that the Most High rules in the kingdom of men, and gives it to whomever He chooses. That very hour the word was fulfilled concerning Nebuchadnezzar; he was driven from men and ate grass like oxen; his body was wet with

the dew of heaven till his hair had grown like eagles' feathers and his nails like birds' claws.

Daniel 4:30-33

King Nebuchadnezzar learnt this important lesson of life the hard and shameful way. At the end of the seven years, his mind was restored and it didn't take him long to humbly accept that all his wisdom, power and riches came from God, not from his own strength. It took him seven tough humbling and degrading years to comprehend this truth I'm sharing with you. Though it's good to learn from the errors of others so as not repeat the same mistakes they made, it's far better to learn from the scriptures by abiding by the instructions and principles God has already given us concerning life. It's wisest to adopt what He loves as our lifestyle and keep a real distance away from what He detests. Knowing and embracing His trademarks for living is the real essence of life.

LIVING WITHOUT REGRETS

"A LIFE NOT LIVED FOR OTHERS IS NOT A LIFE."

MOTHER TERESA

Living from God's perspective is the surest mean means to a life without regrets, and a life without regrets is a life lived for the kingdom. Be kingdom-minded, have a persistent kingdom-focus. Let nothing turn your attention away from the true essence of life and that in which the Lord delights, which is: kindness, justice and righteousness. It's impossible to express these great values without affecting lives positively, because they don't function in isolation but by relating personally and relevantly with people at their point of need.

You have to be wholly committed to influencing people with the kingdom life. Light is a great influence in the midst of darkness, and the Lord Jesus has made you the light of the world. Thus, your essence for living will find its utmost expression in the darkness dominating your city. In the same way darkness provides opportunity for light, the problems in your community are your opportunities for shining the light of solution, and bringing the light others need. This is a sure-way of living without regrets.

When I considered the overwhelming societal ills that oppressed and made mockery of the lives of the people of the Ukraine, issues ranging from domestic violence, alcohol and drug addiction, armed robbery, high abortion rates, escalated divorce rates, coupled with so many who were orphaned, I felt a deep compulsion to pray and fast for several months for the state of the nation, then God began to show me clearly from the scriptures the role I was to play in restoring hope to these precious lives. One of the most vital truths He relayed to my heart was the need to set up social organizations targeted at meeting specific needs of people in the society. Today, we have several hundreds of rehabilitation centers besides over three thousand social organizations bringing succour to the needy and dying in our world. They are so effective that even the government of the nation consults with them on issues they find difficult to effect changes.

Today, some of my pastors, the nation's leaders and our Church members were former drug addicts, thugs, alcoholics, orphans, prostitutes, folks who were formerly victims in life, and now are not only saved, but are saving others, and redeeming their nations from the unfathomable evils that once beset their very lives. These testimonies of changed lives and societal transformations are my simplest definition of living without regrets.

A life without regret is a life lived for others: a life of kindness, righteousness and justice demonstrated relevantly in solving the problems of others. When you live for others, you never die, because the essence of your being keeps on pulsating through the lives of those you've affected.

When you devote yourself to living for others, your life carries on a trans-generational impact, because not only are you affecting lives positively, but posterity to come. Your purpose on earth is to serve people. Your mission in life is to live for others, not yourself. Jesus Christ reiterated this truth when He said that He had come not to be served but serve and give His life as a sacrifice for many. That's Kingdom-driven living: living for others, sacrificing yourself to see them free from the limitations of life. This is what I emphasize in our Church. We raise our members not to think of themselves and their problems, but to think of how to save their nation and invade every field of human endeavour with kingdom values. We help them identify their calling, train them and send them out as saviours to their world.

Don't be self-centred, live for the well-being of others. Aim for their salvation, fulfillment and success. True success isn't defined by the amount of wealth amassed, but by how many lives one has influenced positively. Think about influencing the lives of others, carrying their burdens, extending arms of loving-kindness towards them. Self-centerdness is the bane of the sufferings of many around the world, especially in our African continent. There is already so much evil in the world rooted in man's selfish desires, and the only way to make a difference is to live with a different mindset; the mindset of the kingdom: a mind controlled by love for people; directed with a passion to bring the reign of righteousness and justice to bear upon our society and affairs of men. It's high time you stopped thinking just about yourself, your family, your self-perceived needs but conceive a larger picture: the Kingdom-spread and service to humanity.

A life without regret is that lived for the kingdom. As the Church, we bear the enormous responsibility of permeating every facet of our culture with the lifestyle, values and principles of the Kingdom. You're to invade the darkness of your society with the ever-brightening light of righteous-living. It's quite unfortunate that many Christians today haven't clearly understood the purpose of the Church, and thus have been poor specimens in extending the domain of Christ's kingdom on earth. In fact, some have rather settled for a lifestyle that brings reproach to the Christendom by living egocentric lives, focusing entirely on their needs with little or no interest in the kingdom agenda. You're called to proclaim and spread the Kingdom everywhere: upholding a lifestyle of kindness, righteousness and justice everywhere.

Until the self in you dies, the true leader in you will not arise. Don't live for self; be committed to living for others. Living for others is what makes a success of life.

The man Job became the greatest of all men of his time by serving and living for others. He extended an arm of kindness, righteousness and justice to the people in his world. He was a man with a kingdom-mindset. And as a result, he turned out to become to wealthiest man in his country and time, yet wealth wasn't his primary pursuit; neither was wisdom nor the acquisition of power his focal interest. He was driven by the understanding of what God delights in: kindness, justice and righteousness, which are the essence of life.

There was a man in the land of Uz, whose name was Job; and that man was blameless and upright, and one who feared God and shunned evil. And seven sons and three daughters were born to him. Also, his possessions were seven thousand sheep, three thousand camels, five hundred yoke of oxen, five hundred female donkeys, and a very large household, so that this man was the greatest of all the people of the East.

Job 1:1-3

Job said:

When the ear heard, then it blessed me, and when the eye saw, then it approved me; because I delivered the poor who cried out, the fatherless and the one who had no helper. The blessing of a perishing man came upon me, and I caused the widow's heart to sing for joy. I put on righteousness, and it clothed me; my justice was like a robe and a

turban. I was eyes to the blind, and I was feet to the lame. I was a father to the poor, and I searched out the case that I did not know. I broke the fangs of the wicked, and plucked the victim from his teeth."

Job 29:11-17

What a rich testimony the man Job had of an enduring and impactful kingdom lifestyle, no wonder he was the greatest of the East.

From the scripture above, let's pay a closer attention to the class of people Job demonstrated exceeding kindness to: the poor, widow, orphans, and helpless; the lame, blind, perishing and victims of wickedness. He was eyes to the blind, feet to the lame. He was a father or provider to the poor. He caused the heart of the widow to sing, and the list goes on. He was an upholder of the weak; his kindness made a difference for the fatherless and widows; he stood up in defence of the poor in righteousness; spoke out for the reign of justice.

This is the Gospel of the Kingdom: living to bring the kindness, righteousness and justice of our Master Jesus to bear upon the affairs of men. This is a classic example on how to live without regrets and build a kingdom legacy!

Living for the kingdom positions you in God's greater purpose that spells benefits for humanity and satisfaction in life. You were born for the kingdom: to impart its principles and values to your world. God's main desire is for you to be sold-out to spreading His kingdom in your world. As a believer, not only are you a God-carrier, but a Kingdom-carrier as well, loaded with the virtues of life, to bring a godly influence upon the lives of men and your society.

I'd love to also state here, that to live without regrets, it's essential that you give your very best at every given point in time.

Whatever your hand finds to do, do it with your might; for there is no work or device or knowledge or wisdom in the grave where you are going.

Ecclesiastes 9:10

Give your best, in your marriage, family, church, workplace, and every endeavour of life. Give your best for the kingdom.

"NOBODY WHO EVER GAVE HIS BEST REGRETTED IT."

GEORGE HALAS

God gave His best - the life of His only begotten Son, Jesus Christ to save humanity and redeem the earth from destruction. On that cross, not only did Jesus take away our sins, He also took away the curse sin brought upon the earth, as a crown of thorns was placed on His head. Today God has us as His redeemed-children: the harvest of His best gift as well as the earth: the field that He bought back with the blood of His Son Jesus. He has no regrets for giving His best.

In the same way, give your best for the kingdom and you will have no regrets. Live to give your best every day, and experience a life without regrets!

LIVING WITH PASSION AND ZEAL

"PASSION IS THE GENESIS OF GENIUS."

GALILEO GALILEI

Understanding the essence of life is one thing, but heralding its cause with passion and zeal is another. Life runs on the engine of passion, and the values of the kingdom are spread through zestfulness.

You need to be passionate about life. Death sets in when passion sets out. Life should be characterized by vigour and vitality. Be passionate for the Kingdom. Life without passion is nothing.

Passion is a driving force that propels one towards a set purpose; it is a burning and intense zeal that converts your goals into tangible realities. It makes your goals achievable. Passion isn't a feeling, but an attitude of the mind. You don't have to wait to feel like doing what is right before doing so, rather, do what is right and the feelings will follow.

"WE MUST ACT OUT OF PASSION BEFORE WE CAN FEEL IT."

JEAN-PAUL SARTRE

Someone said do it with passion or not at all. In other words, in devoting our lives to the essence of living, we must be passionate.

Our purpose for living finds expression in a passion-driven life. We need to exert enormous amount of passion in the realization of our kingdom purpose. Nothing of great value was ever achieved in life without a passionate drive, in the same way, to fulfill the essence of life, you need to be passionate.

"LIGHT YOURSELF ON FIRE WITH PASSION AND PEOPLE WILL COME FROM MILES TO WATCH YOU BURN."

JOHN WESLEY

People with great passion can make happen what others term impossible.

This brings to mind a deep thought about my home country, Nigeria, where many have often said: "Only God can save Nigeria." Can you imagine how we have come to mystify our age-long problems with faith-less doubts? Well I wrote a book on this very subject to prove that you as an individual can make a change. Besides other factors, you need to be passionate about this. It takes a burning passion to make a real difference in your world.

Have passion for what you do. Live your life with great passion. Passion drives perfection.

All History Makers were folks burning with intense passion. Thus, your heart of kindness, righteousness and justice must ride on the wheels of passion to bring about positive impacts in the lives of others and in your society at large.

In November 1993, while preparing to begin the Embassy of God (though we began with the name of Word of Faith Church), I was seeking the face of the Lord for the right strategy in reaching the people as well as setting the right goals.

The first goal we set for the growth of the Church was to have 1,000 members within the first two years, and 2,000 in five years. I figured out that if our target was a thousand in the first two years, we ought to work so hard with great passion to achieve it in one year rather. Thus, we needed to double in our efforts and put a system in place to ensure we reached this goal in a period of one year. I thought: "If I wanted to have 1,000 people a year, approximately 100 people should join the church monthly." So we went to work passionately on our goals."

Though I had a team, I didn't rely entirely on their efforts at the beginning; I simply considered theirs an added bonus. Thus, I wasn't only praying and fasting, but was also on the streets and everywhere possible, preaching to people, inviting them with so much passion and conviction. I was extremely zealous about this. I personally invited 30 times more the number of people we targeted for each month and God performed a miracle: 100 people remained in the Church per month as we kept reaching out zealously to the city. By our Second Year Anniversary, we had reached 2,000 members, instead of 1,000 which was our original goal. God was faithful and He more than rewarded our passionate efforts as we exceeded our goals and kept doing so by His grace.

You need to be really passionate about life and accomplishing goals in order to succeed. Passion is what would wake you up to pray, without needing an alarm clock. Passion is what would drive you to reach out to mend the broken lives in your community even when faced with several challenges. Passion is absolutely vital in spreading the kingdom.

"I HAVE NO SPECIAL TALENTS. I AM ONLY PASSIONATELY CURIOUS."

ALBERT EINSTEIN

All over the world today, so many lose their jobs due to a lack of zest and enthusiasm. A recent report on employee survey by The Huffington Post revealed that 88% of employees don't have real passion for their work, and only 20% of senior managers are passionate about their work, thus resulting in a poor contribution of their full potential towards national development. Besides, having a leader that isn't passionate about their work can definitely lead to bad results in terms of employee productivity. In today's rapidly changing business environment, companies need passionate workers to drive extreme and sustained performance needed to overcome various market challenges and disruptions.

In the same way, you need to be absolutely passionate in spreading the values and principles of the kingdom in your world, in order to overcome the various challenges and negative trends opposing the kingdom lifestyle we represent. Don't express a lackadaisical attitude towards life, burn with a kingdom-driven passion and purpose.

This reminds me of the Bible character, Phinehas whose passion and zeal for the kingdom turned away God's wrath from consuming the entire children of Israel when they sinned against Him. He acted with a righteous zeal against those who broke the commandments of the Lord and as a result received God's outright commendation:

Phinehas, son of Eleazar, the son of Aaron the priest, has turned my anger away from the Israelites. Since he was as zealous for my honour among them as I am, I did not put an end to them in my zeal. Therefore tell him I am making my covenant of peace with him.

Numbers 25:11-12

126

Your zeal for the kingdom is the answer to the problems besieging your nation. Don't be lukewarm. It's time to live with enthusiasm and act in passion for the kingdom. Jesus said that the zeal of His Father's house had consumed Him. He was driven by passion to live from God's perspective.

Decide to live from God's perspective by living a passion-driven kingdom life. Spread the values of life in your contacts with people; exalt the values of kindness, justice and righteousness in your sphere of contact.

GOLDEN NUGGETS

1. An important way to keep growing is to never stop asking questions. The person who afraid of asking is afraid of learning.

2. Studying and learning brings approval in life, and to truly live from God's perspective you must humble yourself and become a learner in life.

3. Those who commit to learning and improving themselves will make fewer mistakes in the journey of life than those who don't.

4. When you understand life as a gift, there would be no room for unnecessary boasting or showing off.

5. When you live for others, you never die, because the essence of your being keeps pulsating through the lives of those you have affected.

6. When you devote yourself to living for others, your life carries on a trans-generational impact because not only are you affecting lives positively but posterity to come.

7. Until the self in you dies, the true leader in you will not arise.

8. Life runs on the engine of passion and the values of the kingdom are spread through zestfulness.

CHAPTER 7

LIVING FOR KINDNESS

"LET NO ONE EVER COME TO YOU WITHOUT LEAVING BETTER AND HAPPIER. BE THE LIVING EXPRESSION OF GOD'S KINDNESS: KINDNESS IN YOUR FACE, KINDNESS IN YOUR EYES, KINDNESS IN YOUR SMILE."

MOTHER TERESA

The true essence of life is becoming the very living expression of God's kindness. When you devote yourself to loving and showing kindness to people, you manifest the God-life on the earth. His nature becomes visible and tangible through our acts and words of kindness. God is kind, and as His son or daughter, you have this same nature in you. Thus, you are to express it in your dealings with people.

Kindness is one of the foremost manifestations of God's heart of love:

Love is kind

1 Corinthians 13:4

His kindness is what triggered the gift of His Son, Jesus Christ as sacrifice for our sins. He was kind to an unkind world; selfless in giving to a selfish world. This is the nature of the God of the Universe: loving-kindness!

This is the reason He wants us to be kind, as He is and fill our respective societies with indomitable deeds of kindness. Kindness can break-through the hardest of heart and soften the toughest of all, because it's a language everyone understands and needs, no matter their culture, race or religion.

Mark Twain said:

"KINDNESS IS THE LANGUAGE WHICH THE DEAF CAN HEAR AND THE BLIND CAN SEE."

That's absolutely true!

Every individual deserves your kindness, even if he or she gave you the worst of all treatments. Kindness is a constant demand God places on our relationships and contacts with people, even those we aren't acquainted with, because when you act kindly you reflect the kingdom of God. In fact, be kind to unkind people. They need it most.

Kindness is one word that simply defines what it means to be kingdom-minded. When your heart is full of the consciousness of the kingdom, your thoughts, words and deeds will naturally translate into acts of kindness.

"IF YOU WANT TO LIFT YOURSELF UP, LIFT UP SOMEONE ELSE"

BOOKER T. WASHINGTON

Many years ago, I felt it was impossible to be kind to every single person. But I discovered the secret of how to do it and today, I can boldly say that there is no person I don't like. I really do love all people. I arrived at that place of loving-kindness through a difficult realization. One day God told me to listen to my own sermons on tape because I was teaching principles that I didn't fully embody. So I put all my sermons together and began listening to them and reading through all my notes. I started memorizing the Word and meditating on it.

During one particular two-month period I concentrated on 1 Corinthians 13, the love chapter. I prayed and meditated over it. I knew in theory that love is not provoked, yet I was often provoked. I meditated on how to apply that revelation in different situations. I asked myself, "What if someone punches me or spits into my face? Will I be provoked then? I found out that my knowledge was still theory, so I took the Word again and "replayed" it in my mind until theory was transformed into practice. By the time I finished that exercise, I found I had become a different person. I could no longer be provoked. I grew to love not only the members of my church but also my enemies and those who plotted evil against me. I can now boast that there is no one I don't like in my life. That love-nature of God has produced in me an ability to love and be kind to everyone irrespective of who they are and what they've done.

KINDNESS IS MORE THAN DEEDS. IT IS AN ATTITUDE, AN EXPRESSION, A LOOK, A TOUCH. IT IS ANYTHING THAT LIFTS ANOTHER PERSON.

PLATO

As followers of King Jesus, we are to embody the nature of our King in order to manifest His kingdom in every sphere of our human endeavour. When you manifest kindness, you manifest the kingdom. No wonder, kindness is seen in God's eyes as a legitimate cause for boasting:

> **This is what the Lord says: "Let not the wise boast of their wisdom or the strong boast of their strength or the rich boast of their riches, but let the one who boasts boast about this: that they have the understanding to know me, that I am the Lord, who exercises kindness, justice and righteousness on earth, for in these I delight, "declares the Lord.**
>
> *Jeremiah 9:23-24*

Your boast in life shouldn't be in how many fleet of cars you own, houses you've built, certificates you've acquired, but in your understanding of the Lord and expressions of His kindness. In other words, how many people have you helped? Whose education have you sponsored? How many have you led to Christ? How kind are you to those who are cruel towards you? How many have you helped who could never pay back? Who have you given assistance to at their moment of greatest need? That's where real boasting lies. But in real sense, our boasts are not really to be vocalized by us, but our actions. As actions speak louder than words, so does your kindness demonstrate the reality of Christ and His kingdom of love to those in your world!

Many things in this world will come to an end, and cease to be relevant, but deeds of kindness never die. Unlike the mundane things of life that fades out with time, loving-kindness does not cease on earth. It remains as a seed that brings forth endless harvests. It surpasses the earth to reach the heaven. So it is to anyone that devotes his life into showing loving-kindness. When you are committed to a kingdom lifestyle of showing kindness to people, you'd experience the limitless power of God in your life and live a life of unfading success.

THE SUPERLATIVE VALUE OF KINDNESS

"YOUR WEALTH OR STATUS DOESN'T MAKE YOU. YOUR KINDNESS AND CHARACTER DOES."

VENKAT DESIREDDY

Another most important reason you need to devote your life to being kind towards people is because kindness is of superlative value when compared with wisdom, wealth or power. Kindness is superior to these alluring factors many crave for in life. Its value is so great that God equates Himself with it:

He who does not love does not know God, for God is love.

1 John 4:8

God is Love. He is not wisdom, but He's Omniscient; He is not Power, but He's Omnipotent; He doesn't equate Himself with Riches, but owns all things. The only thing He equates Himself with is Love, and love is kind. Thus any man who is manifesting kindness is operating at the highest plane of love; He's functioning with the understanding of God.

When you treat people with kindness, you're demonstrating the love-nature of God and spreading His kingdom values in the world of men, and this is His utmost desire.

In the Old Testament, the term lovingkindness, which is a combination of two words in our modern language today, is often used in qualifying the character of God. These two words are actually inseparable: Love and kindness – Lovingkindness. You cannot love and not be kind and you cannot be kind and not love. It is a twin word that reflects the nature of God Himself.

Kindness is loving people more than they deserve. God loves us and treats us with lovingkindness, more than we deserve. This is what He wants us to do to others today. Don't be kind only to those who are kind to you, be kind as well to unkind people, they need it the most. The true measure of an individual is how he treats a person who can't pay back. Love and show kindness to people before you ever try to influence them. The law of connection states that leaders touch a heart before they ask for a hand. When you move their hearts with emotion, you can then move them to action. Jesus Christ who is the greatest of all leaders showed peter so much kindness by helping him launch out into the deep for a great draught before calling Peter to follow him (Luke 5:1-11). Peter followed Jesus all the way.

Unconditional love is what draws people to God and keeps them growing in the Kingdom. The Church grows stronger when we demonstrate kindness in practical ways towards people. Remember, what really count is how well our character reflects Christ to the world.

Thus, being kingdom-minded is manifesting kindness purposefully in life.

BREAKTHROUGHS OF LOVINGKINDNESS

"THE SMALLEST ACT OF KINDNESS IS WORTH MORE THAN THE GRANDEST INTENTION"

OSCAR WILDE

People have often asked how my breakthrough in ministry started. It wasn't in learning and absorbing the Russian culture and language, though this gave me invaluable tools. It wasn't learning how to preach or feel comfortable ministering before a group. No. My breakthrough came when I left the pulpit and went to the streets to look for the outcasts.

Honestly, I never even knew such people lived in Kyiv in any substantial numbers. I had always kept myself with university students and other so-called ordinary people. I didn't know there was a whole world of drunkards, drug addicts, and forgotten people living in the shadows of society.

But when I reached out to them with arms of lovingkindness, doors opened up wide for ministry. Someone in our church knew of a hospital where drunkards were kept, so I began to go there and beg the doctors to give me one hour to be with the patients. I would bring along Natasha, one of our ministers today, who testified how she was delivered from alcoholism, and then I prayed for the patients. There, my ministry kicked off. God began to honour that sacrifice with supernatural anointing.

When I prayed for drunkards and addicts they would suddenly wake up from their stupor. The power of God would descend on them so strongly that they would be set free in an instant. As a result they began to come to church. Then their mothers would come asking, "What did you do to my son? We spent everything to try to help him. We don't care if you're red, white, or black. You've given us back our son." In one year the church grew to a thousand people, and the Lord added a thousand to us every year after that. We changed meeting places six times in one year, going from east to west to south to north of the city. But it didn't matter anymore. I knew I had the key. Lovingkindness! If I could manifest God's lovingkindness towards this people, I could change the world!

When you start serving people radically with love, you open them up to the kindness of the Saviour and life of the Kingdom. Our kingdom influence spreads on the wings of lovingkindness. Therefore, be kind to people. Never let a day end without showing profuse kindness towards people. Devote yourself to acts of kindness for this is the essence of life.

A Story of Lovingkindness

"THREE THINGS IN HUMAN LIFE ARE IMPORTANT; THE FIRST IS TO BE KIND. THE SECOND IS TO BE KIND. THE THIRD IS TO BE KIND."

Mother Teresa

When I envisage living without regrets, what comes to mind first is a life wholly devoted to knowing the Lord and practicing the values of the kingdom which include lovingkindness, righteousness and justice.

The life story of Mother Teresa's remains quite fascinating to me because it plays out the literal meaning of the scripture we've repeatedly emphasized.

Mother Teresa was born August 26, 1910, in Skopje, the current capital of the Republic of Macedonia. The following day, she was baptized as Agnes Gonxha Bojaxhiu. Her parents, Nikola and Dranafile Bojaxjiu, were of Albania descent; her father was an entrepreneur who worked as a construction contractor and a trader of medicines and other goods. The Bojaxhius were devoutly Catholic family, and Nikola was deeply involved in the local church as well as in city politics as a vocal proponent of Albanian Independence.

In 1919, when Agnes was only 8 years old, her father suddenly fell ill and died. While the cause of the death remains unknown, many have speculated that political enemies poisoned him. In the aftermath of her father's death, Agnes became extraordinarily close to her mother, a pious and compassionate woman who instilled in her daughter a deep commitment to charity.

Although by no means wealthy, Drana Bojaxhiu extended an open invitation to the city's destitute to dine with her family. *"My child, never eat a single mouthful unless you are sharing it with others,"* she counselled her daughter. When Agnes asked who the people eating with them were, her mother uniformly responded, "Some of them are our relations, but all of them are our people." I strongly believe that by these acts of kindness Drana

Bojaxhiu extended to the poor in their community, she planted seeds of destiny in her daughter that would become great oaks of succour to a dying world.

When she was aged 12, along with her congregation, they embarked on a pilgrimage to the Church of the Black Madonna in Letnice. During these pilgrimage trips is when young Agnes first felt within herself a call to be a missionary. Then exactly six year later, 1928, the 18-year-old decided to become a nun and set off for Ireland to join the Sisters of Loreto in Dublin. That was where she adopted the name Sister Teresa.

Shortly after a year, Sister Teresa travelled on to Darjeeling, India and was later transferred to Calcutta, where she was assigned to teach at Saint Mary's High School for Girls, a school run by the Loreto Sisters and dedicated to teaching girls from the city's poorest Bengali families. There, Sister Teresa learned to speak both Bengali and Hindi fluently as she taught geography and history and dedicated herself wholly to alleviating the girl's poverty through education. After her Final Profession of Vows, she took on the title of "Mother" and became known as Mother Teresa, as she continued to teach at the School and sooner was made the Principal of the same institution. Through her kindness, generosity, and unfailing commitment to her students' education, she sought to lead them to a life of devotion to Christ. *"Give me the strength to be ever the light of their lives, so that I may lead them at least to you,"* she wrote in prayer.

However, on September 10, 1946, Mother Teresa experienced a second calling, the "call within a call" that would forever transform her life. She was riding a train from Calcutta to the Himalayan foothills for a retreat when she said Christ spoke to her and told her to abandon teaching to work in the slums of Calcutta aiding the city's poorest and sickest people.

But since Mother Teresa had taken a vow of obedience, she could not leave her convent without official permission. After nearly a year and a half of lobbying, in January 1948 she finally received approval to pursue this new calling. That August, donning the blue-and-white sari that she would wear in public for the rest of her life, she left the Loreto convent and wandered out into the city. After six months of basic medical training, she voyaged for the first time into Calcutta's slums with no more specific a goal than to aid "the unwanted, the unloved, the uncared for."

Mother Teresa quickly translated this somewhat vague calling into concrete actions to help the city's poor. She began an open-air school and established a home for the dying destitute in a dilapidated building she convinced the government to donate to her cause. In October 1950, she won canonical recognition for a new congregation, the Missionaries of Charity, which she founded with only a handful of members - most of them former teachers, or pupils from St. Mary's school.

As the ranks of her congregation swelled and donations poured in from around India and the globe, the scope of Mother Teresa's charitable activities expanded exponentially. Over the course of the 1950s and 1960s, she established a leper colony, an orphanage, a nursing home, a family clinic, and a string of mobile health clinics.

In 1971, Mother Teresa travelled to New York City to open her first American-based house of charity, and in the summer of 1992, she secretly went to Beirut, Lebanon, where she crossed between Christians East Beirut and Muslim West Beirut to aid children of both faiths. In 1979, she was awarded the Nobel Peace Prize in recognition of her work "in bringing help to suffering humanity."

In 1985, Mother Teresa returned to New York City and spoke at the 40th anniversary of the United Nations General Assembly. While there, she also opened Gift of Love, a home to care for those infected with HIV/AIDS.

By the time of her death in 1997, the Missionaries of Charity numbered more than 4,000 - in addition to thousands more lay volunteers - with 610 foundations in 123 countries around the world!

Here was a story of life laden with kindness. Though she's long gone, her kingdom impact remains felt not only in India, but all over the world. She poured in all her life for others.

Who are you living for?

What diligent efforts are you making today to manifest the lovingkindness of the heavenly Kingdom in your society?

I challenge you today, to arise from mere existence to true living. Devote yourself to a life of kindness.

I often hear people say they have chosen not to show kindness again because their previous acts of kindness was trampled on by others. Never give up on kindness. It's better to make mistakes in kindness like Mother Teresa said.

"I WOULD RATHER MAKE MISTAKES IN KINDNESS AND COMPASSION THAN WORK MIRACLES IN UNKINDNESS AND HARD-NESS."

MOTHER TERESA

Love is the greatest force in the universe. Give it to your world. Make a daily habit of showing kindness to your world. Look for opportunities to be kind to people. You can help an aged woman carry some load on the street, you can pass some knowledge you have to some other folks that can benefit from it, you can give food to the hungry, helps to the poor, comforting someone that needs to be comforted, you can visit the sick, prisoners and help liberate those in all forms of captivity. This indeed is the true gospel. People that show kindness with their gifting will be fulfilled in life. They will also receive the Lord's commendation on judgement day (Mathew 25).

GOLDEN NUGGETS

1. Kindness is the language which the deaf can hear and the blind can see.

2. Kindness is a constant demand God places on our relationships and contact with people, even those we aren't acquainted with because when you act kindly, you reflect the kingdom of God.

3. The true measure of an individual is how he treats a person who can't pay back.

4. When you treat people with kindness, you are demonstrating the love-nature of God and spreading His Kingdom values in the world.

5. Kindness is of superlative value when compared with wisdom, wealth and power.

CHAPTER 8

LIVING FOR JUSTICE

JUSTICE CONSISTS NOT IN BEING NEUTRAL
BETWEEN RIGHT AND WRONG, BUT IN
FINDING OUT THE RIGHT AND UPHOLDING
IT, WHEREVER FOUND, AGAINST THE
WRONG."

THEODORE ROOSEVELT

HE LIVED AND DIED FOR JUSTICE

On 4 April 1968, Dr. Martin Luther King was shot
dead in Memphis, Tennessee, where he planned to lead
a protest march. The powerful voice of Dr. King was
silenced, but almost fifty years later, his ideas are still
a source of inspiration for people who seek peace and
justice.

He was a Baptist minister and social activist who
played a key role in the American civil rights movement
from the mid-1950s until his assassination. Inspired by
advocates of nonviolence such as Mahatma Gandhi, King
sought equality for African Americans, the economically
disadvantaged and victims of injustice through peaceful
protest. He was a driving force behind watershed events
such as Montgomery Bus Boycott and the March on
Washington, which helped bring about such landmark
legislation as the Civil Rights Act of 1964 and the Voting
Rights Act of 1965. King was awarded the Nobel Peace

Prize in 1964 and is remembered each year on Martin Luther King Jr. Day, a U. S federal holiday since 1986.

The second child of Martin Luther King Sr., a pastor, and Alberta Williams King, a former schoolteacher, Martin Luther King Jr. was born in Atlanta, Georgia, on January 15, 1929. Along with his older sister, the future Christine King Farris, and younger brother, Alfred Daniel Williams King, he grew up in the city's Sweet Auburn neighbourhood, then home to some of the most prominent and prosperous African Americans in the country.

> INJUSTICE ANYWHERE IS A THREAT TO JUSTICE EVERYWHERE."
>
> MARTIN LUTHER KING JNR.

A gifted student, King attended segregated public schools and at the age of 15 was admitted to Morehouse College, the alma mater of both his father and maternal grandfather, where he studied medicine and law. Although he had not intended to follow in his father's footsteps by joining the ministry, he changed his mind under the mentorship of Morehouse president, Dr. Benjamin Mays, an influential theologian and outspoken advocate for racial equality. After graduating in 1948, King entered Crozer Theological Seminary in Pennsylvania, where he earned a Bachelor of Divinity degree, won a prestigious fellowship and was elected in a predominantly white senior class.

King then enrolled in a graduate program at Boston University, completing his coursework in 1953 and earning a doctorate in systematic theology two years later. While in Boston he met Coretta Scott, a young singer from Alabama who was studying at the New England Conservatory of Music. The couple wed in 1953 and settled in Montgomery Alabama, where King became pastor of the Dexter Avenue Baptist Church. They had four children.

The King family had been living in Montgomery for less than a year when the highly segregated city became the epicenter of the burgeoning struggle for civil rights in America, galvanized by the landmark Brown v. Board of Education of Topeka decision of 1954. On December 1, 1955, Rosa Parks, a secretary of the local National Association for the Advancement of Coloured People Chapter, refused to give up her seat to a white passenger on a Montgomery bus and was arrested. Activists coordinated a bus boycott that would continue for 381 days, placing a severe economic strain on the public transit system and downtown business owners. They chose Martin Luther King Jr. as the protest's leader and official spokesman.

By the time the Supreme Court ruled segregated seating on public buses unconstitutional in November 1956, King heavily influenced by Mahatma Gandhi and the activist Bayard Rustin, had entered the national spotlight as an inspirational proponent of organized, nonviolent resistance. He had become a target for white supremacists, who firebombed his family home that January. Emboldened by the boycott's success, in 1957 he and other civil rights activists-most of them fellow ministers-founded the Southern Christian Leadership Conference (SCLC), a group committed to achieving full equality for African Americans through nonviolence. Its motto was *"Not one hair of one head of one person should be harmed."* He would remain at the helm of this influential organization until his death.

In his time as SCLC president, Martin Luther King Jr. travelled across the country and around the world, giving lectures on nonviolent protest and civil rights as well as meeting with religious figures, activists and political leaders. During a month-long trip to India in 1959, he had the opportunity to meet family members and followers of Gandhi, the man he described in his autobiography as "the guiding light of our technique of nonviolent social change." King also authored several books and articles during this time.

In 1960 King and his family moved to Atlanta, his native city, where he joined his father as co-pastor of the Ebenezer Baptist Church. This new position did not stop King and his SLCL colleagues from becoming key players in many of the most significant civil rights battles of the 1960s. Their philosophy of nonviolence was put to a particular severe test during the Birmingham campaign of 1963, in which activists used a boycott, sit-ins and marches to protest segregation, unfair hiring practices and other injustices in one of America's most racially divided cities. Arrested for his involvement on April 12, King penned the civil rights manifesto known as the "Letter from Birmingham Jail," an eloquent defence of civil disobedience addressed to a group of white clergymen who had criticized his tactics.

"YOU MAY CHOOSE TO LOOK THE OTHER WAY BUT YOU CAN NEVER SAY AGAIN THAT YOU DID NOT KNOW"

WILLIAM WILBERFORCE

Later that year, Martin Luther King Jr. worked with a number of civil rights and religious groups to organize the March on Washington for jobs and freedom, a peaceful political rally designed to shed light on the injustices African American continued to face across the country. Held on August 28 and attended by some 200,000 to 300,000 participants, the event is widely regarded as a watershed moment in the history of the American civil rights movement and a factor in the passage of the Civil Rights Acts of 1964.

The March culminated in King's most famous address, known as the "I Have a Dream" speech, a spirited call for peace and equality that many consider a masterpiece of rhetoric. Standing on the steps of the Lincoln Memorial monument to the president who a century earlier had brought down the institution of slavery in the United States - he shared his vision of a future in which "this nation would rise up and live out the true meaning of its creed: 'We hold these truths to be self-evident, that all men are created equal.'" The speech and march cemented King's reputation at home and abroad; later that year he was named Man of the Year by TIME magazine and in 1964 became the youngest person ever awarded the Nobel Peace Prize.

In the spring of 1965, King's elevated profile drew international attention to the violence that erupted between white segregationists and peaceful demonstrators in Selma, Alabama, where SCLC and Student Nonviolent Coordinating Committee (SNCC) had organized a voter registration campaign. Captured on television, the brutal scene outraged many Americans and inspired supporters from across the country to gather in

Selma and take part in a march to Montgomery led by King and supported by President Lyndon Johnson, who sent in federal troops to keep the peace. That August, Congress passed the Voting Rights Act, which guaranteed the right to vote-first awarded by the 15th Amendment – to all African Americans.

> "OUR LIVES BEGIN TO END THE DAY WE BECOME SILENT ABOUT THE THINGS THAT MATTER."
>
> MARTIN LUTHER KING JR.

This quote above can be reversed as this: our lives are lived well when we don't keep silent about the things that matter. In 1967, King and the SCLC embarked on an ambitious program known as the Poor People's Campaign, which was to include a massive march on the capital.

> "I HAVE A DREAM THAT MY FOUR CHILDREN WILL ONE DAY LIVE IN A NATION WHERE THEY WILL NOT BE JUDGED BY THE COLOUR OF THEIR SKIN BUT BY THE CONTENT OF THEIR CHARACTER"
>
> MARTIN LUTHER KING JR. "I HAVE A DREAM" SPEECH, AUGUST 28, 1963.

On the evening of April 4, 1968, King was fatally shot while standing on the balcony of a motel in Memphis, where he had travelled to support a sanitation workers' strike. In the wake of his death, a wave of riots swept major cities across the country, while President Johnson declared a national day of mourning. James Earl Ray, an escaped convict and known racist, pleaded guilty to the murder and was sentenced to 99 years in prison.

After years of campaigning by activists, members of Congress and Coretta Scott King, among others, in 1983 President Ronald Reagan signed a bill creating a U.S federal holiday in honour of King, observed on the third Monday of January, for a man who lived and died for justice to prevail: Martin Luther King Jr.

THE THEORY OF JUSTICE

An authoritative definition of justice is elusive, the meaning of justice varies. In simple terms it denotes equity, fairness, impartialness, or lack of prejudice; fairness in protection of right and punishment of wrong.

In ordinary parlance, law and justice are synonymous. However justice is the correct application of a law, as opposed to arbitrariness. Law is therefore not an end but a means to an end. That end is justice. Thus, it would be misleading to assume that the concept of justice means the same thing to everybody. Obviously, the word would mean different things to plaintiff and defender, rich and poor, students and teachers, etc. Justice is the philosophical and legal theory by which fairness is administered. Justice to all men is a moral standard of all men, requiring them to perform their moral or social obligation to one another and grant each other what they fairly deserve.

There are various theories of justice, but we will major in summary on only two here.

First being, Formal Justice: a theory which postulates that the court must apply law strictly without any regard to any extra-legal considerations. In other words, the judge is bound to give effect to the law as it is and has no discretionary power to mitigate its harshness.

Secondly, the Substantive Justice: which requires that where the strict application of the law produce absurdity or injustice, the judge may consider some extra judicial factors in interpreting the law in order to arrive at a jurist decision.

But what really is the essence of justice?

Etymologically, Justice comes from the Latin word, "Jus" meaning right. It is the fairness in the protection of right and punishment of wrongs. Justice is important in the society because not everybody would love to be obedient in the society, thus, justice which is fairness in punishing acts will play its part and cause people to do what's right to avoid being punished. Moreover, justice helps to create a safe environment where people live in, and relate with respect to law and order. Thus, we can boldly say that the opposite of justice is not injustice but a lack of love in the society, for justice is the love of the truth!

JUSTICE: TRUTH IN ACTION

"I SAY THAT JUSTICE IS TRUTH IN ACTION"

BENJAMIN DISRAELI

Justice is truth in action.

God delights in justice and greatly detests the prevalence of injustice. Giving your life for the reign of justice is identifying yourself with the essence of life. Martin Luther King Jr. lived to bring justice amidst a world of segregation and unfair practices. And the reason his legacy lives on more than fifty years after his departure is because he was upholding a kingdom cause: a purpose greater than himself - the will of God. Committing yourself to rightly defending the truth wherever it is opposed would definitely make you an enemy of evil and darkness, but light is greater than darkness; truth is superior is lie. God is Light, we are His light in this dark world, thus, wherever we are, He expects us to shine, not hide or be silent about the evil occurrence in our midst.

Joseph in the Bible was hated by some of his brothers because he stood for what was right, he was just. He didn't pretend not to be oblivious of the malicious and uncanny deeds his brothers were involved in, but spoke against their unbecoming behaviour, and made honest reports of these to Israel his father. His stance for justice is what made him endearing and trustworthy to his father. When his brothers became envious of him and his dreams, and decided to harm him, God miraculously intervened, in saving his life and he ended up sold a slave; a slave who later became prime minister of Egypt, the most powerful nation of the time. But these began when he took an uncompromising stand for the truth.

I also believe that his understanding and firm resolution to do what was right, speak for the truth even when his elder brothers were breaking the laws, was due to the training and mentorship Israel, his father had given him. He took good advantage of the wealth of knowledge, experience and understanding his great father, a patriarch of faith and valued the principles of life he learnt of him, allowing those truths form the fabric of his character and integrity. He was a true mentee and son of his father. Little wonder when sold into Egypt as a slave, to Potiphar the Captain of Pharaoh's guard, who set him as overseer and administrator of his house, when he was tempted by Potiphar's wife to have sex with her, he wouldn't compromise his values and faith in God. His new position didn't cause him to forget the laws of God regarding how life should be lived. He saw God as the God of justice and wouldn't attempt to break his principles of life. At the end of the day, Joseph was justified by God and exalted to the highest office in that same land, because he stood his ground on the truth and lived a life of integrity.

COMPASSION IS NO SUBSTITUTE FOR JUSTICE

Knowing what justice means also necessitates knowing what it isn't. Compassion is no substitute for justice. It is not a replacement for justice. Though God is Love; He is also just; therefore wrong must be fully judged and right duly rewarded. Sin must be atoned for and righteousness exalted. Thus, the offering of His Son Jesus Christ to die on the cross for our sins was a manifest demonstration of His unconditional love and righteous justice. Love in the sense that God gave His only begotten Son as the atoning sacrifice of man's sins; justice in the sense that Jesus was judged for all our sinful deeds and died on a cross because the wages of sin is death.

His love never beclouds His justice, and His justice never undermines His love. He is Love and a God of justice, and we need both. We belong to a Kingdom where love and justice reigns, and thus need to be people of love, and at the same time, uphold justice in all our endeavours.

Can you imagine a society without justice, where evil reigns and wickedness goes unpunished or even unquestioned? Such would be a society without foundations, a place of endless tragedies and pains; nation heading for horrible destruction. But thank God for justice: the enforcement of truth and order. In fact love functions through justice, and flourishes in the knowledge of the truth. The knowledge of the truth places on us a sense of responsibility to uphold it at all times, especially in the face of injustice and abuse of power.

"COMPASSION IS NO SUBSTITUTE FOR JUSTICE"

RUSH LIMBAUGH

In our society today, there are so many soft-minded, quiet, compromising Christians, who don't want to interrupt the evils going in their world. They say, "let sleeping dogs lie," in other words, let's mind our business and not interfere. But acting this way makes you a partner or supporter of the evil that's going on. Someone rightly said: "Evil prevails when righteous men do nothing."

We have to do something; we need to rise up to defend the weak and poor; and free the oppressed from the clutches of the wicked. We need to uphold the kingdom values of justice and honesty against the appalling rise of corruption in every sphere of our society. Injustice anywhere is indeed a threat to everywhere.

If you choose to be silent or quiet today about the evil that's going on in your city, one day, you may become the victim of that evil. If we don't stand against these evil deeds, our children might become victims of them in the future. We have been called to devote our lives for justice to prevail. Don't be compromising. Stand for something. Take a solid stand for the truth. Those who stand for nothing fall for nothing. Be a person of character and integrity. Don't be swayed by the currents of corruption and new trends of deceptions common in our world, uphold the truth and it will uphold you.

When Queen Esther thought she could be silent about the impending doom and holocaust her fellow Jews could face by the hands of wicked Haman, their enemy, Mordecai quickly passed on a vital message to her, reminding her that God had brought her into that privileged office of Queen to defend His people and promote the sovereign cause of His Kingdom at such a time as that. Thank God she mounted up real courage and stood up in defence of the Kingdom.

What do you stand for? What are you living for today? Remember time is life, and in a short while we will all leave this world, but before we do, we must take a stand. In fact, our eternity and rewards after this earthly journey will be based on how we stood up to oppose evil and proclaim the truth; how we upheld righteousness and tore down the walls of wickedness. You will be rewarded on earth and in eternity for your stance on justice.

The problem with our nation is that we have too many lukewarm Christians: believers who just want to prosper on earth and make it safely to heaven. That sounds just like what Queen Esther could have imagined: staying silently and safely in the royal palace without creating a scene or drawing attention.

But thank God she didn't, because her boldness and stance on the truth saved several thousands of life and preserved posterity.

As followers of Jesus Christ, we must walk in his footsteps and imitate His examples. Jesus Christ was indeed the Lord of justice. He stood for the truth to the extent that He gave His life as a sacrifice for the truth. That's why He had enemies: those who hate the truth. In the book of Hebrews 1:6-7, the scriptures described Him as loving righteousness and hating wickedness, therefore God had exalted His throne to the highest place of honour for all eternity, because He pursued and gave His life in exchange for justice.

God hates lukewarm-Christianity. In fact He even prefers you to be rather hot or cold than to being merely lukewarm - in between the two, having one leg here and one leg there, doing a little good and being complacent with evil. That's not the life of the Kingdom; that's not how life works.

"A SALVATION THAT DOES NOT LEAD TO SERVICE IS NO SALVATION AT ALL"

CATHERINE BOOTH

Give yourself for a righteous cause: be a person of justice. Do what is right and have the courage to resist what is wrong. Your commitment to doing what is right shouldn't be based on who is watching, but the fact that it is the right thing to be done. It doesn't matter the enemies you may make, it doesn't matter the friends you may lose. What matters is that you have understood the value of life and will not give yours in exchange for evil, but good and righteousness. No matter the critics that rise against you in your effort to uphold justice, they will never prevail, because greater is He that is in you, than he that is in the world. The God of justice whose truth you uphold be it in your office, school, church, work place, family, wherever in your sphere of contact, will speak for you and defend you as you defend His truth.

WE MUST CONTEND EARNESTLY FOR THE TRUTH THAT HAS BEEN DELIVERED TO US, CHOOSING WHAT IS RIGHT OVER WRONG.

We must contend earnestly for the faith that has been delivered to us, choosing what is right over wrong. Let the truth you've understood become pivotal in your decision-making and day to day living. Every day is a gift from God as it affords you an opportunity to build your character and devotion to the truth, so that when the deceptive allurements of life present themselves, your mind wouldn't be enticed and carried away from the truth.

BE DEVOTED TO A LIFE OF JUSTICE

God calls Himself a God of Justice. If God Almighty would identify with this dimension of life, meaning that He attaches His life and reputation to align with justice. Then anyone of our lives would do good to be dedicated to such a cause. Justice is worth giving one's life for. Don't give your life for riches or wealth; it is of lesser value. The idea of bribery and corruption is as old as time itself, where people sell off their integrity and conscience for temporary riches or desires. Even though it's a common practice today in our nation, we shouldn't indulge in it. You shouldn't bribe your way into a public office, to get a job or an admission to the University; you ought not to bribe your way to passing an exam. That equates selling your destiny or devaluing yourself. You are more than whatever money can buy. Don't sell cheap. Maintain your value and uphold the cause of justice. Life is more than riches. We need to fight against misdeeds such as bribery and corruption.

This reminds me of when the Religious leaders in the time of our Lord Jesus Christ bribed the Roman soldiers who were to guard the tomb of his burial site, to spread a fallacious report, stating that the body of our Saviour was stolen by his disciples, because they the Lord had risen from the dead. He was no longer in the tomb! Though their mouths were shut by bribery and corruption, our mouths are widely open to proclaim justice that He is risen, alive and He is Lord of heaven and earth! Their efforts to forestall the truth didn't work and will never be able to stop the spread of the Kingdom.

In order words, standing for the truth will put you on the winning side of life for all seasons of life. You will have an inward peace and satisfaction that knows no bounds for doing what is right, saying what was right and defending the truth despite the opposition you faced. Nothing is sweeter than truth, mixed with grace and upheld in words and just deeds. Dedicate yourself to the cause of justice.

JUSTICE: A CREDIBLE CAUSE OF BOASTING

Justice is a credible cause of boasting according to God. A life devoted to bringing justice, advancing justice and establishing justice is often superior to wisdom, power or wealth.

Friend, I want you to know that God takes pleasure in Justice, He delights in it. It flexes his muscles. So also God takes pleasure in any man who devotes His life to advancing the cause of justice. This is the kind of value, life is worth living for.

Give yourself purposefully to the advancement of justice wherever you find yourself at any given point in time, and you'll see God promoting you to higher levels in life, because a heart of justice is a heart of humility; a heart that exalts the truth and principles of the kingdom above all human prejudice.

"A MAN WHO WON'T DIE FOR SOMETHING IS NOT FIT TO LIVE."

MARTIN LUTHER KINGJR.

God is no respecter of persons. He has exalted His word or principles above all things. So when you exalt His principle of justice in your dealings with men, He will see to it that you experience an unstoppable advancement in life. He will personally push you forward and open doors to expand your influence for His kingdom sake. He will cause you to shine brighter and brighter, so that His truths will reign:

The path of the just is as the shining light, that shines more and more unto the perfect day

Proverbs 4:18

Heaven is in dire need of just men; just men made perfect; just men who have grown into the full knowledge of who they are and what they are here for.

God needs just men, men He can entrust with greater responsibilities; men who can control the helm of affairs and run the kingdom with fairness and truth; men who would willingly risk their lives to uphold justice and truth.

Are you such a person?

Are you available?

Men of character are scarce in every nation of the earth. They are assets to the nations they live in. Men of integrity with a heart to do justice are in high demand. Be a person of value. Your worth in life is in the strength of your character; your esteem of kingdom values and practice of His principles. Develop yourself in these truths and become a person of real value, so that you can carry out God's agenda for your life on earth.

Francis Bacon said: *"If we do not maintain justice, justice will not maintain us."*

Don't forget life is all about service and justice is a form of service to humanity. The justice you uphold today will not only uphold you in days to come, but your posterity and generation as well. Maintain the cause of justice wherever you are and never compromise the truth. Defend the truth and the truth will defend you. Uphold the truth and it will uphold you.

"JUSTICE IS A CONSCIENCE, NOT A PERSONAL CONSCIENCE BUT THE CONSCIENCE OF THE WHOLE HUMANITY."

ALEXANDER SOLZHENISTYN

Let's rise up and speak against injustice wherever it surfaces itself in our sphere of influence. Don't tolerate wickedness due to the fear of man; don't pretend to be unaware of wickedness when it doesn't affect you. Stand up against it without prejudice. The scripture says, resist the devil and he will flee from you. If the devil flees at our resistance, then injustice, which is a form of his several manifestations, is surer to flee at our solid stance and resistance. If you resist injustice, it will flee from you.

What we tolerate is what continues. What we permit is what prevails. What we condone is what controls. But when we disallow something, it loses its power to operate freely in our presence.

This is exactly what Jesus meant, when He spoke of the keys of the Kingdom:

> **I give unto you the keys of the kingdom, and whatsoever you shall bind on earth, shall be bound in heaven, and whatsoever you shall loose on earth shall be loosed in heaven**
>
> *Matthew 16:19*

In the Christendom, we love to apply this scripture in regards to casting out demons and evil spirits from people and domains. But it bears a wider kingdom application and relevance, especially regarding the concept of justice.

Firstly, let's be reminded that Jesus was talking about the kingdom here: how to spread its domain and extend its access to men everywhere. That's the reason He specifically talked about keys of the kingdom. Besides, keys denote authority, power and access. Thus, when He said that He's given us the keys of the Kingdom: that whatsoever we bind or disallow on earth shall be bound or disallowed in heaven and whatever we lose or permit on earth shall be loosed or permitted in heaven. In the actual rendering, it says that whatever you bind on earth, is what has been bound in heaven, and whatever you loose on earth, is what has been loosed in heaven. This corresponds with our Lord's Prayer: "your will be done on earth as it is in heaven." So when you know what is done, permitted or loosed in heaven; you are to ensure it is done, permitted or loosed on earth. And when you get to know through the knowledge of the scriptures what is bound, not permitted or disallowed in heaven, you are to ensure it is bound, not permitted and disallowed on earth. And God has placed you in office for this cause.

God has placed us in charge of the earth for this cause. We are His representatives, vice regents and ambassadors of His Kingdom on earth, to administrate His righteous cause and ensure the reign of His truth and justice. You have been authorized; you have your orders!

Through the knowledge of the scriptures, we get to fully understand what to bind on earth and what to loose on earth. Take for instance there is no form of injustice, corruption, or prejudice in heaven; in the same way, disallow all forms of injustice from manifesting in your sphere of influence. You have the kingdom right and authority to forestall resist injustice in your own sphere of influence. Rise to your calling and be devoted to this cause.

Let Justice Reign

"YOU WILL HAVE FEWER REGRETS IN LIFE IF YOU START FOCUSING AND TAKING RESPONSIBILITY FOR WHERE YOU ARE AND WHERE YOU WANT TO BE."

DEBORAH DAY

Life is all about taking responsibility. Stop blaming others for the present situation of things, rise and take up responsibility, do what is just where ever you are.

Learn to stand up for what is right even if you're standing alone. In reality, you aren't because you are surrounded by the truth that never fails. Take responsibility to uphold the truth wherever you are.

Where you are today is the starting point. Begin from where you are. When you're faithful in little things, God will entrust you with greater opportunities. Be a person of character, upholding the truth and the truth will surely uphold you.

GOLDEN NUGGET

1. Our lives begin to end the day we become silent about the things that matter.

2. Giving your life for the reign of justice is identifying yourself with the essence of life.

3. Love functions through justice and flourishes in knowledge of the truth.

4. If you choose to be silent or quiet today about the evil going on in your city, one day, you may become the victim of that evil.

5. You will be rewarded on earth and in eternity for your stance on justice.

6. You will have an inward peace and satisfaction that knows no bound for doing what is right and defending the truth

CHAPTER 9

LIVING FOR RIGHTEOUSNESS

Righteousness exalts a nation, But sin is a reproach to any people.

Proverbs 14:34

God's final choice of values for which life could be sacrificed is righteousness. Devote your life to a righteous cause. True righteousness is more than a self-conscious admiration of one's sin-less state, but a desperate hunger and thirst to carry out righteous acts aimed at improving the lot of humanity.

The scripture says:

Blessed are those who hunger and thirst for righteousness, for they shall be filled.

Matthew 5:6

True righteousness has a hunger. It is characterized by a thirst to see the enthronement of truth.

It takes an insatiable hunger to birth righteousness in any nation. We must first be thirsty if we will live to see the defeat of age-long evils and corrupt practices that have been a persistent limitation to the growth and advancement of our nation. There can be no enthronement of righteousness in our nation without first a burning thirst in our hearts.

In reference to righteousness and the kingdom, our Lord Jesus said:

> **For I say to you, that unless your righteousness exceeds the righteousness of the scribes and Pharisees, you will by no means enter the kingdom of heaven.**
>
> *Matthew 5:20*

If we will experience the reign of God's righteousness and dominion of His kingdom in our community or nation to the extent where armed robbery gets on the lowest decline; where kidnapping of innocent lives for ransom becomes obsolete; where cultism and occultic practices no longer exist in our institutions of learning; where bribery and corruption becomes a thing of the past; where stealing of public funds is brought to criminal justice; where prostitution, unemployment and all unfair practices are effaced, our righteousness must first exceed the righteousness of the scribes and Pharisees.

You cannot experience the full measure of life and peace that comes from the righteous reign of God's kingdom in your heart and in your world, until you lay aside self-righteous and embrace the God-kind of righteousness. The scribes and the Pharisees were known for the self-righteous boasting of how righteous their deeds were. They boasted of how much they prayed and fasted, yet their prayers changed nothing. They boasted of how much they tithed every single money and possession, yet their tithing didn't get God's attention because it was devoid of true righteousness and mercy. They boasted of their spiritual heritage of being sons of Abraham, yet were secretly planning the crucifixion of their Savior, Jesus.

Charles Spurgeon said:

"THE GREATEST ENEMY TO HUMAN SOUL IS THE SELF-RIGHTEOUS SPIRIT WHICH MAKES MEN TO LOOK TO THEMSELVES FOR SALVATION."

How true!

The righteousness that comes by faith derives its confidence from a relationship with God, not mainly one's pious deeds. It is the hunger for righteousness that starts us on the path of making history and becoming His agents of national transformation.

PURE CHRIST-LIKE LOVE FLOWING FROM TRUE RIGHTEOUSNESS CAN CHANGE THE WORLD."

JEFFREY R. HOLLAND

Every time I set myself aside in prayer retreats to be alone with God, I am simply increasing my thirst to see His righteousness and bring His kingdom to bear upon the affairs of men in my world. The world around is full of so much coldness towards God; an unreasonable thirst for prevalence of wicked works and it has a way causing us to lose our passion and appetite for God's presence and the spread of His kingdom on earth. That's the reason we must learn to daily and routinely create time for God and spend quality time with Him in order to refuel our zeal for a righteous invasion of His truth on earth.

The righteous will be remembered forever.

Psalm 112:6

Embrace the righteousness of God and manifest it in your sphere of contact. Manifest it in your marriage, family, school, office, community and everywhere you go. Righteousness is not a garment we put on to Church on Sundays, and then put off during week-days; it's an upright life we live daily before God.

Righteousness is a lifestyle: a kingdom-lifestyle that mustn't only permeate our human relationships but dominate the culture of our society. It's our kingdom culture, and God expects us to super-impose this culture in our sphere of influence. He wants to see you bring His righteousness into the economy of your nation and defeat the strongholds of recession and unemployment, like Joseph did. He wants to see you invade the health sector of your government with righteous medical ethics and practices in your hospital or health centers that upholds the kingdom.

I learnt that gifted youngsters these days, who're Christians, are afraid of singing songs that exalt kingdom values and the praise of God, for fear of not making good sales or promotion. So these young musicians resort to songs that focus on gangsters, immorality, and wealth; ignoring the essential values of life.

That's unfortunate!

We need to restore the reign of righteousness and give our lives for the kingdom. That is where our true fulfillment and prosperity as individuals and a nation will rise from.

Jesus said:

> **But seek first the kingdom of God and his righteousness, then all these things will be added unto you**
>
> *Matthew 6:33*

In your life's pursuit, what comes first to you, what is your priority? Is it success, fame, riches, and popularity? Have a honest assessment of your heart and be sure these aren't your principal pursuits or motives in life, because if they are, your heart is not right with God and His kingdom, and these transient desires will not only drown you but destroy your life and all you ever esteemed.

The kingdom path of righteousness isn't based on covetousness, greed or selfishness, but it surely culminates in all the good things of life we desire with present and eternal benefits, because when we pursue the well-being of others, our well-being cannot be lost.

WHAT IS RIGHTEOUSNESS?

Righteousness refers to our right-standing with God; the nature of God that separates a person from evil and makes him or her just in God's sight. It is a divine passion to do right and seek the wellbeing of your fellow human being. It is pursing the forceful and gracious advancement of kingdom purposes in your sphere of influence.

True righteousness is not a passive state, but an active force. A force that drives you on your knees in prayer; a thrust that keeps you awake cogitating on how to overcome the evil in your world with good; a spirit that gives you no rest until all is done to restore the reign of truth in your society. That's righteousness.

It is very true that righteousness is that divine nature of God we receive at the new birth that grants us boldness to fellowship in God's presence without guilt and makes us right in His sight; the divine ability to be right and do what is right, just and acceptable."

For if by the one man's offense death reigned through the one, much more those who receive abundance of grace and of the gift of righteousness will reign in life through the One, Jesus Christ.

Romans 5:17

This righteous-nature we have of God in Christ Jesus isn't meant just for singing, dancing, praising and thanking God for the forgiveness of our sins. No, there's more that God intended by giving us His own very nature of righteousness and clothing us with it.

THE GOAL OF RIGHTEOUSNESS IS THE REIGN OF THE KINGDOM OF GOD ON EARTH.

The goal of righteousness is the reign of the kingdom of God on earth. By receiving the salvation of Christ and His gift of righteousness, we are responsible for restoring the reign of righteousness and eradicating every evil that dishonors our Savior-King.

If you have received abundance of grace and God's gift of righteousness, you ought to reign in life by applying the principles and values of our King Jesus and our Kingdom in your sphere of life.

Righteousness is more than a struggle to stop sinning. What impresses God is not your righteousness, because He made you His righteousness in Christ, in the first place.

What righteous cause of the kingdom are you committed to or upholding in your community? What are you doing to push away the darkness in your society? What steps are you taking to alleviate poverty and hunger strikes that's become a norm in your neighborhood? You need to put your gift of righteousness to work to affect lives positively.

"WHAT WE DO IN LIFE ECHOES IN ETERNITY."

MAXIMUS

Listen friend, we have to do more than sharing Church invitation cards or gospel tracts? We have to go an extra mile in loving the people at their desperate point of need unto salvation. We must identify their needs and bring tangible gospel solutions. That's manifesting righteousness!

Greater love has no one than this, than to lay down one's life for his friends.

John 15:13

Jesus laid down His life for us and the whole world at a time when we were without help; and He did so in righteousness. Righteousness is laying down your life to save the life of another person in need:

God demonstrated His righteous love by sacrificing the life of His only begotten Son to set us free from our bondage of sin and eternal damnation. He manifested His righteousness. He didn't stop at proclaiming righteousness; He went the extra mile to manifest it. And He has charged us with the same responsibility to manifest righteousness towards people in their time of greatest need and overcome the evil that has plagued our world:

...Because He laid down His life for us... we also ought to lay down our lives for the brethren.

1 John 3:16

We ought to lay down our lives for our brothers and sisters; families and friends; nation and society. This is the true kingdom righteousness. This is the only way to defeat evil and enthrone righteousness. There is no other way. This is what Jesus meant when He said that anybody who desires to be His disciple must deny himself, take up his cross and follow Him. Taking up your cross is devoting yourself to His righteous cause; it denotes sacrificing your life for His righteous cause; favoring His will at any cost.

FAVOR HIS RIGHTEOUS CAUSE

Let them shout for joy and be glad, Who favor my righteous cause; And let them say continually, "Let the LORD be magnified, Who has pleasure in the prosperity of His servant.

Psalm 35:27

The true essence of life is devoting oneself in favor of the righteous cause of the kingdom. When you live with this mindset, success in life becomes inevitable, and failure impossible, because your commitment to God's success makes Him wholly committed to your own success in life. Besides, His will becomes your will. Such was the experience and testimony of William and Catherine Booth, the founders of the world renowned Salvation Army.

When asked for the secret of his success, William Booth said: "I will tell you the secret. God has had all there was of me. There have been men with greater brains than I, men with greater opportunities. But from the day I got the poor of London on my heart and caught a vision of all Jesus Christ could do with them, on that day I made up my mind that God would have all of William Booth there was. And if there is anything of power in the Salvation Army today, it is because God has had all the adoration of my heart, all the power of my will, and all the influence of my life."

What a devotion to righteousness!

This man and his beloved wife were sold out to meeting a specific need in their immediate environment with the gospel of the Kingdom. They identified with the poor and took up the responsibility to catering for their needs, and though hundreds of years have passed, yet their work remains in existence. That's success in life.

True success isn't the kind that fades out with the exit of the key-man, but lingers on in legacy and deeds through generations to come. And such can only be possible if your motive and pursuit was the righteous cause of the kingdom.

Writing about his father, William said: "My father was a Grab, a Get. He had been born into poverty. He determined to grow rich; and he did. He grew very rich, because he lived without God and simply worked for money; and when he lost it all, his heart broke with it, and he died miserably."

Born 10 April, 1829, he had three sisters and an elder brother who died on his second birthday. When he was aged 13, his father sent him to work as an apprentice to Francis Eames in a pawnbroker's shop situated in the poorest part of Nottingham. He disliked his job, but it was through this work that his social conscience was stirred and he became aware of the plight of the poor.

In September that same year, his father Samuel became ill and died, shortly after repentance and acceptance of Christ. Not long after, his mother had to leave the house in Sneinton for a shop in one of the poor quarters of Nottingham where she earned a meager income selling toys, needles, cotton and the like.

It was at this time, that William started attending Broad Street Wesley Chapel, and in 1844 he had a conversion experience.

In the way of righteousness there is life, along that path is immortality.

Proverbs 12:28

Soon after Booth's conversion, one day, he brought a group of poor, rugged boys from the slums into the church. Instead of being pleased, the minister was angry and Booth was told next time to bring them through the back door and seat them where they couldn't be seen. As he feared, the Church of his day was becoming too "respectable." His long hours in the pawnshop stretched out for six years and though he often worked until 8pm, he would hurry to prayer meetings which would last until 10pm. Sometimes after this, he would call on the sick and dying. It is said that he made hundreds of hospital calls before he was twenty years of age. He also did much street preaching late at night during these years.

Working with the outcasts and poor of Nottingham brought increased burdens for the larger cities. Seeing London in 1849 at the age twenty, he said, "What a city to save!" Sixteen years later he began to help save it. That was July 2nd, 1865 when the Salvation Army started, and William screamed: "I have found my destiny!" Then onwards, converts streamed to the tent.

> "EACH OF US HAS MEANING AND WE BRING IT TO LIFE. IT IS A WASTE TO BE ASKING THE QUESTION WHEN YOU ARE THE ANSWER."
>
> JOSEPH CAMPBELL

Once in an outburst of concern for the lost, he exclaimed, "Oh God, what can I say? Souls! Souls! Souls! My heart hungers for souls!" As he grew old and eyesight became weak he went for operation. Two days later it was found that he had an infection and that he would lose his sight completely. Then he said: "God knows best. I have done what I could for God and the people with my eyes. Now I must do what I can for God and the people without my eyes."

What a dedication to righteousness and the kingdom in spite of a failing health condition!

By the time of his death over two million had given their lives to Christ, nations all over were transformed by this singular general and so many enlisted into the kingdom army of spreading God's righteous cause on earth.

I challenge you today, to favor His righteous cause. Identify a problem in your immediate community or a sphere in your nation and devote your life to seeing the righteousness of God prevail over it. William and Catherine Booth went for the poor and transformed a nation. Look inwards, where lies your burning desire, passion and thirst? Go all out and commit yourself to bringing the reign of righteousness to the meet the needs of people in your world. Start where you are, one person at a time is all it takes to make a difference. Favor His righteous cause!

Don't be a man pleaser, don't try to be at peace with men at the expense of imparting righteousness in your world. Stand for the righteousness you have received.

"IF I MUST CHOOSE BETWEEN RIGHTEOUS-NESS AND PEACE, I CHOOSE RIGHTEOUS-NESS."

THEODORE ROOSEVELT

Some people condescend from their stand of righteousness at their work places and societal groups they are involved in just to please their colleagues. For instance, they may tell you, let's all sign that we used a thousand coins and apparently all that was used was five hundred coins. You may not have an inside peace to sign it with them but some people will sign that to be at peace with men at the extent of their stand for righteousness. Always stand for righteousness no matter what it costs. That's the true fulfillment of life.

ENDURING EFFECTS OF RIGHTEOUSNESS

Until the Spirit is poured upon us from on high, and the wilderness becomes a fruitful field, and the fruitful field is counted as a forest. Then justice will dwell in the wilderness, And righteousness remain in the fruitful field. The work of righteousness will be peace, and the effect of righteousness, quietness and assurance forever. My people will dwell in a peaceful habitation, in secure dwellings, and in quiet resting places, though hail comes down on the forest, and the city is brought low in humiliation. Blessed are you who sow beside all waters, who send out freely the feet of the ox and the donkey.

Isaiah 32:15-20

One of the most beneficial and enduring effects of righteousness is a life of fruitfulness, peace, quietness and assurance forever. When you devote your life to bringing about righteousness in your career, business, relationships or finances, you will enjoy endless peace and there will be nothing to make you afraid.

He who follows righteousness and mercy finds life, righteousness and honor.

Proverbs 21:21

When you choose to deal honestly with your business partners, not using false measures or cheating, your peace and prosperity will be as sure as the sunshine. There are folks who are afraid of dealing honestly in business; they think the only way to make profit is by cheating other. But that's not the way of righteousness. The divine nature in you must pervade every facet of your endeavor to better the lot of humanity.

Don't be afraid of doing what is right even when you're the only person doing so. Being popular isn't what matters, but doing right. Get ready to sow your life and devote yourself in righteousness. Sow yourself as a seed of righteousness to your generation.

At salvation and the baptism of the Holy Spirit, we received both a righteous nature and the Spirit of righteousness, not just to fold our arms, sing some hymns, carry out a few church chores and be a nice Christian fellow. You received the Spirit of righteousness to bring forth fruits in your society. You have been mandated to convert the wilderness or unfruitful sectors of your nation's economy into a fruitful field or effective sectors, and the fruitful or effective field to a forest or super-efficient fields. You are anointed to make a difference in the market place.

One of the most important effects of righteousness is fruitfulness. Fruitfulness is simply obtaining results, achieving set-purposes; when things are working the way they are expected to work, we say it's fruitful. Therefore your presence in your office should make things work there!

"TRUE RELIGION IS REAL LIVING; LIVING WITH ALL ONE'S SOUL, WITH ALL ONE'S GOODNESS AND RIGHTEOUSNESS."

ALBERT EINSTEIN

It baffles me when I consider the fact that we have so many committed Christians in our nation and sectors such as electric power supply is yet to attain satisfactory working conditions, needless to mention our agriculture or mining industry, even our educational system needs a total revamp if we are going to educate and train youths with information tailored for real nation-building.

Our nation needs sons of the kingdom. The world is waiting not for the manifestation of children, but manifestation of sons, because it is sons who can manifest and demonstrate righteousness. It is sons who can save. It's high time we stopped being babyish and selfish Christians and start thinking about rebuilding our nation, looking beyond all religious and ethnic discriminations; but capturing a vision for our future and devoting our lives sacrificially until righteousness, justice and peace is enthroned in our nation. It's high time we began sowing our lives beside all waters, identifying an area in our society and pouring our lives to bring in the righteous values of the kingdom for then will our nation and people prosper. Then will we enjoy the enduring effects of righteousness, peace and unshakable prosperity.

ORGANIZED RIGHTEOUSNESS

For Zion's sake I will not hold My peace, And for Jerusalem's sake I will not rest, Until her righteousness goes forth as brightness, And her salvation as a lamp that burns.

Isaiah 62:1

By the term "organized righteousness" I'm referring to putting the righteousness of God in you to work in a way that solves a problem in your society and meets a human need.

It is unleashing that divine nature in you towards birthing societal transformation. This is what we need!

Genuine righteousness is never passive; it's an active force, a thrust that cannot be stopped; a fire that cannot be quenched; a passion that cannot be contained. We are responsible for channeling this fiery fire of righteousness in meeting the needs of our generation.

Righteousness involves seeking the well-being of our fellow human beings. Let's lay aside our religious coats and embrace the true value and essence of our lives.

We have heard of lots of collapsed buildings in our beloved country Nigeria. Most of these occurrences are as a result of materials that are below the required standards for the buildings. This happens on account of selfishness and unrighteous deeds for example a contract for a five storey building was awarded at a cost of three hundred million naira, the cost price to have met the standard requirements for the building would be two hundred and ninety million naira. The contractors would all have had a good profit of ten million naira but instead, low quality products of a hundred and fifty million naira was used for the building all so they would go back home with excessive cash that they didn't labour for. This definitely reduces the durability and efficiency of the building. The care for the wellbeing of those that would stay in the building isn't there. All they care about is their belly. The building eventually collapsed and people died. There was no one to have stood for righteousness.

Let us be the change we desire in our world. You can make a huge difference by standing for righteousness. Let us get rid of bribery, corruption and every unrighteous acts, think about the people that could be affected negatively by it, and have genuine love for God and people.

Imagine this alarming story I heard happened in Nigeria, some top people in government were given a contract to do ten boreholes in some destitute local government villages in the country where people were dying daily of bad water intake. In a quest to embezzle money, they dug just three boreholes and these three didn't extend to some of the villages. People were getting sick and dying daily. The cries of many were being heard yet the selfishness of men didn't move them to use the opportunities given to them to help preserve the lives of many.

Live your life to execute righteousness.

A life of righteousness is that which is given to proclaiming, advancing and establishing God's righteous cause on the earth, and such a life is His delight. Don't give your life in exchange for wealth, wisdom or power. Devote your life for the reign of righteousness in your nation.

For the kingdom of God is not eating and drinking, but righteousness and peace and joy in the Holy Spirit.

Romans 14:17

Remember, God is not impressed by your self-righteousness, but by the righteousness of your movement. In other words, how you convert that righteous nature He's placed within your heart to bettering the cause of humanity and ease the sufferings of others. But for us to succeed at doing this, we must be well organized. Righteousness must be organized.

"HOW CAN WE EXPECT RIGHTEOUSNESS TO PREVAIL WHEN THERE IS HARDLY ANYONE WILLING TO GIVE HIMSELF UP INDIVIDUALLY TO A RIGHTEOUS CAUSE. SUCH A FINE, SUNNY DAY, AND I HAVE TO GO, BUT WHAT DOES MY DEATH MATTER, IF THROUGH US, THOUSANDS OF PEOPLE ARE AWAKENED AND STIRRED TO ACTION?"

SOPHIE SCHOLL

I would love to round off this chapter of ours by making a brief reference to a touching story of Sophia Scholl, a German student who sacrificed her life in righteousness to oppose the evil works of Adolf Hitler and the Nazi party which killed 11 million people during the Holocaust of which 1.1 million were children, and 6 million of those victims were Jewish.

Sophia Scholl was a German student, who was active in the White Rose - a non-violent resistance group to

Hitler and the Nazi party. In 1943, she was caught delivering anti-war propaganda and, with her brother Hans Scholl, was executed for high treason. She has become an important symbol of anti-Nazi resistance in German. A Lutheran Christian by upbringing, she dedicated her early and brief life in Christ to opposing the heinous works of Adolf Hitler. For years, she went around spreading and posting thousands of leaflets containing vital information to sensitize the public and people of Germany against the wicked plans and inhuman ideology of the Nazi party. During her interrogation before execution by the army, she said:

"I AM, NOW AS BEFORE, OF THE OPINION THAT I DID THE BEST THAT I COULD DO FOR MY NATION. I THEREFORE DO NOT REGRET MY CONDUCT AND WILL BEAR THE CONSEQUENCES THAT RESULT FROM MY CONDUCT."

Sophia Scholl gave her life in exchange for the kingdom, to manifest righteousness in her nation, and today, that truth she upheld reigns!

What will you give your life for? If you haven't discovered what you are willing to die for, then you haven't discovered what you're willing to live for.

God is counting on us to solve the problems in our respective nations, that is the reason He placed us there in the first place. Heaven is looking out to see what we will do, and the earth is crying out; many are desperately in need of help. Don't shut your ears to their cries. Let the pains and struggles of others become yours as well. Identify with the sufferings of others and make meaningful contributions in their lives. If there are no problems where you are today; if there is no darkness where you are right now, it means you have no opportunities to shine the light of righteousness to bring faith, hope and love to the hearts of others. Refuse to remain an ordinary person. Jesus came to make you a history maker. Ordinary people focus on solving their problems, but History makers focus on solving national problems. Ordinary people waste time criticizing government, but History makers set up and execute Non-Governmental Organizations (NGOs) or Social Projects to solve a societal problem. Heroes are not born, they are made. You are born to be a hero for the kingdom. Accept the clarion call. Embrace a righteous cause and manifest righteousness in your world today!

GOLDEN NUGGETS

1. It takes an insatiable hunger to birth righteousness in a place. You must be hungry for righteousness.

2. There can be no enthronement of righteousness in our nation, without first a burning thirst in our hearts.

3. The greatest enemy of human soul is the self righteous spirit which makes men to look to themselves for salvation.

4. The goal of righteousness is the reign of the kingdom of God on earth.

5. Righteousness is laying down your life to save the life of another person in need.

6. Start where you are, one person at a time is all it takes to make a difference.

7. Don't be afraid of doing what is right even when you are the only person doing so.

8. A life of righteousness is that which is given to proclaiming, advancing and establishing God's righteous cause on earth

CHAPTER 10

THE TRUE ESSENCE AND VALUE OF LIFE

"IF YOU WANT TO IDENTIFY ME, ASK ME NOT WHERE I LIVE, OR WHAT I LIKE TO EAT, OR HOW I COMB MY HAIR, BUT ASK ME WHAT I AM LIVING FOR, IN DETAIL, ASK ME WHAT I THINK IS KEEPING ME FROM LIVING FULLY FOR THE THING I WANT TO LIVE FOR."

THOMAS MERTON

As we gradually conclude on this most important subject, which bears quintessential value for all who live, will live and yearn to live life, in its fullest, purest and truest form, I wish to bring your attention again to the very thoughts and will of our Creator God on the essence and value of your life: what He expects life to be for you, His design for your life and how to actualize it. The scripture contains the heart and mind of God, His eternal will and purpose for humanity and society. It's the safest and most reliable source of truth to depend on regarding life. It says:

This is what the Lord says: "Let not the wise boast of their wisdom or the strong boast of their strength or the rich boast of their riches, but let the one who boasts boast about this: that they have the understanding

to know me, that I am the Lord, who exercises kindness, justice and righteousness on earth, for in these I delight, "declares the Lord."

Jeremiah 9:23-24

Access to maximizing your life's journey on earth has been given to you. Now, you have the keys of life in your hands, and can open up the doors to an endless life of joy and fulfillment. All that matters hence is what you will do with the invaluable truths you've assimilated and embraced.

Life is not a mystery.

The knowledge of the truth concerning life has made you free from the fears and uncertainties that lie in minds of the ignorant. You have the keys of knowledge: access to information to live a transcendent life that would speak for generations to come. You can make a global difference from where you are. You can transform a city and turn the history of your nation around. Your destiny is now in your palms. If nothing changes hence, it is because you placed no value on what you heard or refused to take action on the truths you've been exposed to. Very few folks on earth know what you've now discovered; thus not many may experience the quality of life you would have if you apply these principles of life.

"IF YOU LIVE FOR THE APPROVAL OF OTHERS, YOU WILL DIE BY THEIR REJECTION."

RICK WARREN

You are here on earth for a reason, and that reason is greater than all your challenges.

THE TRUE ESSENCE AND VALUE OF LIFE

Therefore, refuse to live an ordinary life anymore. Don't condescend to mediocrity or cut-corners in your journey. It's time to sit up and be serious about life.

It's time to arise and shine because your light has come. Before a plane air-lift, the pilot informs the passengers to sit up and put on their seat belts, because it's time to fly. In the same way, it's time sit up, to fly high and soar to new dimensions, so you need to make quality assessment of how you've been living life and what adjustments you need to make in order to reach new heights you've envisioned.

WHAT WILL YOU DEVOTE YOUR LIFE TO?

What will you live for?
What will your days on earth be devoted to?
Life is time; time is in seconds; and your seconds are ticking as we speak. Your devotions today will determine destiny forever. A young man who sits on a computer devouring his time in watching pornography is investing in death and destroying the very essence of his life. What you do with your 24 hours can predict how your life will turn out in 24 years. Life is Predictable. I discovered it, live it and wrote a beautiful book about it. I encourage you to get a copy and secure your future through the understanding of the principles of life contained there.

When I became 33 years old, God had enabled me to become the pastor of the largest church in the whole of Europe and I had fulfilled most of my goals, because the Kingdom of God is the essence of my life. I had to set new goals! God's intention is to transform your life, your promised land, and your nation, and to use you to bring back the earth to Himself, just as He is doing with us in Ukraine.

The truths I'm sharing with you are timeless, ageless and fadeless. They work in every nation and culture; they work for any individual who applies them irrespective of age, gender or race. They are divine principles of the kingdom-driven life.

God in His infinite wisdom knew the alluring effect of wisdom, power and riches could have on us. He knew that these very factors if misappropriated will cause cataclysmic destruction to lives, families, nations and could potentially wipe out a generation. This is absolutely true. If you doubt it, ask the residents of the Japanese cities of Hiroshima and Nagasaki what happened when the United States dropped nuclear weapons on their territories on August 6 and 9, 1945 during the final stages of World War II, which killed at least 129,000 people.

No wonder God instructs us very succinctly not to devote our lives to power or strength. He doesn't want you devoting the entirety of your being towards the acquisition of power: whether it is spiritual power, physical power, political power, media power or economic power. Don't live for power-intoxication. Though power in any form makes things possible, its usage must be guided by the knowledge of God and kingdom values of kindness, justice and righteousness, otherwise it's sure to bring fatal destruction. In our world today, many seek significance through power and folks will do anything to either get power or be around power.

This is a reason behind the kidnappings and ritual killings that are common in our country especially during times of elections and political campaigns. The lust for power has led many to destroy and annihilate innocent lives. This has to stop!

There is no value in destroying a human life for political, spiritual or any form of power at all. Life is greater in value than power.

I felt terribly sad when I hear of many young folks in our nation Nigeria today, commonly known as "Yahoo Boys," who dabble in Internet fraud to deceive several innocent people and steal away their money. Based on news report, in June 5, 2012, a Federal High Court sentenced a certain 'Imonina Kingsley,' of the University of Ilorin, to 20 years' imprisonment for defrauding an Australian of $1,000 by presenting himself as a gay person from the Republic of Benin.

Can you imagine that?

This is just one among the several thousands of such devotion to wealth. Don't devote your life to riches; don't give your soul in exchange for wealth, because:

Wealth obtained by fraud dwindles, but the one who gathers by labor increases it.

Proverbs 13:11 NASB

Wealth gained through fraudulent or get-rich-quick schemes quickly disappears; but wealth obtained from hard work grows over time.

It's even sadder to know that some get involved in fetish practices involving sacrifice of human life to get rich!

The domineering and controlling influence of money and wealth is so undeniably overwhelming, so much that the Lord Jesus Christ himself had to describe it as a god on its own. Money and wealth wields so much influence in our world that it tends to command religious devotion. No wonder, Jesus said: you have to choose whom you would ascribe your devotion or worship to. Would it be God Almighty or mammon – the god of money?

Money seeks to be worshiped, just as much as God seeks true worshippers. Devoting yourself in worship of mammon is a most dangerous place to be in. Don't sacrifice your life for wealth; neither should you make riches your boast in life.

"THE PURPOSE OF LIFE IS A LIFE OF PURPOSE."

ROBERT BYRNE

Life is more than riches. Your life is more valuable than houses, cars or landed properties. Don't allow the challenges of today cause you to trade your beautiful future and eternal destiny. Don't compromise your values for riches, because life is greater than that.

Further, wisdom is alluring another force God commands that we mustn't devote our lives to neither boast of. Don't give your soul in exchange for wisdom. A typical example was when Adam and Eve chose to disobey God's standing order: to desist from eating of the tree of knowledge of good and evil, because the devil beguiled Eve to believe that eating from that forbidden tree, which God said they shouldn't eat from would make them wise, in fact as wise as God. Isn't that foolish? How could one tree make you as wise as the Creator who made all things? A lust for wisdom led to man's rebellious fall.

Wisdom is a good thing; in fact it's a principal factor in life. We all need wisdom. The Bible tells us to get wisdom and with all our getting, get understanding

THE TRUE ESSENCE AND VALUE OF LIFE

alongside with too. The main issue arises when wisdom becomes the ultimate devotion of your life; when it takes your worship; when your quest for it displaces your value of God, His command, principles and values of life. Then that's a big problem! It's too expensive a deal to make, because your value in life is greater than wisdom.

World over, people are running helter-skelter in search of these three: Wisdom, Power and Wealth. Come to think of it, if anyone truly possesses wisdom, he would be set to rule and reign on the earth. We know that kings reign by wisdom. Yet as powerful as it is, God the Author of life is saying that wisdom is not good enough for boasting – talk less of giving one's life in exchange for it. Whew! What a humbling assertion that is!!!

These factors: wisdom, riches and strength shouldn't become the main devotion of your life. Don't be allured or swayed by the seductive power they bear. Don't make it your boast. That's what the Author of Life says. God doesn't want you to fix your heart in these things, as they would detract from the true path of life and make you disregard the true essence of life.

The main way to overcome these distractions and traps of life is to devote yourself to what is greater.

What is greater? What should be the devotion of our lives?

The scripture answers:

"This is what the Lord says: "Let not the wise boast of their wisdom or the strong boast of their strength or the rich boast of their riches, but let the one who boasts boast about this: that they have the understanding

to know me, that I am the Lord, who exercises kindness, justice and righteousness on earth, for in these I delight, "declares the Lord."

Jeremiah 9:23-24

The earnest attachment and profound devotion of your life should be to know the Lord and understand His kindness, justice and righteousness, in order to exercise these virtues in your journey of life. Your depth of this understanding is what will mark you out for distinction on earth and in eternity to come.

Life on earth is but a dot in eternity.

What you do today can affect how you spend eternity. God's instruction concerning how life should be lived is in exalting the values of kindness, justice and righteousness in our dealings with men on earth. This is what He delights in; this is what gets His attention. When you delight in what God delights, your life on earth can be nothing short of a delight!

LIVE A PARADISIACAL LIFE EVERYDAY

There are folks who are waiting to get to heaven before they can live a great, successful and happy life. You don't have to endure life, you can enjoy it. Jesus came so we can have life to the full and enjoy it every day. I believe Jesus lived the best and most fulfilling life on earth. He lived life in its fullest measure, in all its essence and value, because He lived in devotion to God and His kingdom. That's why He could bold assert:

But seek first the kingdom of God and His righteousness, and all these things shall be added to you.

Matthew 6:33

Jesus made the Kingdom His priority, and as a result He lived the most exciting life there is: a paradisiacal life. He devoted Himself to knowing the Father, promoting His righteous cause; His values of lovingkindness, justice and righteousness in every single human relationship and endeavor of life. Jesus is our Number One Model on how life ought to be lived. He came not only to save us, but to show us the way of life; to unveil the true essence and value of life to humanity. He was the One who said that life is more riches, wealth and all the needs our anxious minds could ever desire. He proved that life is more than wisdom or power, when He laid aside His garment and bowed low to wash the feet of His disciples. He went even further to sacrificing His life unto death in a most gruesome way, by crucifixion: in service to God and humanity.

He showed us that life is really about serving people in kindness, justice and righteousness. This is the pathway of life: the true essence and value of life. That by giving away your life, you get it back, by offering yourself to meet the needs of men righteously in your nation, you get to truly live!

I admonish you to choose the real essence of life and pour your life into that which never fades: the Kingdom of God. Live for the kingdom, breathe for the kingdom and pour your life and all into it. That's the way to a paradisiacal life: an unqualified committal of oneself to the spread of kingdom values in the spheres of our society.

YOUR FOCUS MATTERS

What you see could affect what you think and eventually do. What you keep thinking about can affect what direction your life heads towards. To keep heading in the right direction, you need to preserve your focus by fixing your mind always on the essence for being alive on earth.

"LORD, STAMP ETERNITY ON MY EYEBALLS"

JONATHAN EDWARD

What a prayer!

When your focus bears the eternal imprints of the kingdom, your essence for living would be singular.

"WHEN YOUR FOCUS BEARS THE ETERNAL IMPRINTS OF THE KINGDOM, YOUR ESSENCE FOR LIVING WOULD BE SINGULAR."

Let the kingdom spread be your focus each day, think it, eat it, sleep it, preach it, live it, read it and sacrifice your life for it. Organize your time, relationships and every singular endeavour around this all important essence of life. Protect your kingdom-focus for living on purpose.

Let your focus and attention be sold out to what matters the most: the true essence of life, which is the knowledge of God, kindness, justice and righteousness. All human endeavors should promote the knowledge of God, Lovingkindness, Justice and Righteousness.

In actual fact wisdom, makes sense only when it is used to promote the above values. Power makes sense

THE TRUE ESSENCE AND VALUE OF LIFE

only when it is used to promote the above values. Wealth makes sense only when it is used to promote the values of knowing God, establishing lovingkindness, promoting justice and proclaiming righteousness.

> **He has shown you, O man, what is good; And what does the LORD require of you But to do justly, To love mercy, And to walk humbly with your God?**
>
> *Micah 6:8*

If God is to reign on earth, He would only reign by and through the knowledge of God, lovingkindness, justice and righteousness. God would only establish His kingdom on the earth through men and women who are sold out to spreading the knowledge of God, His love and kindness, justice and righteousness.

Thus, our very lives are meant to be devoted to the advancement of these very values and principles of the Kingdom. God Himself delights in the knowledge of His Word, lovingkindness, justice and righteousness covering the earth, thus, as His beloved child, let this become your delight and the primary focus of your life.

THE GLORIOUS ESSENCE OF LIFE

> **For the earth shall be filled with the knowledge of the glory of the LORD, as the waters cover the sea.**
>
> *Habakkuk 2:14*

God's primary reason for bringing us into this world is so we can fill and replenish the earth with the knowledge of the glory of the Lord.

He wants that glory of the kingdom to dominate the heart of every man, and reign in every sphere of our human endeavours. He wants our respective societies established on kingdom values of kindness, justice, and righteousness. And this of course encompasses all other virtues of honesty, generosity, integrity, and benevolent rule.

His desire is that churches in our respective nations would become the true pillars and supports of the truth: by raising sons of the Kingdom and sending them into various sectors and spheres of the society for national transformation, extending the domain of our Lord's kingdom on earth. The role of the Church must be understood from God's perspective, as a vehicle for extending and expanding kingdom influence on earth; a well unveiling His will for humanity.

God's will is for the earth to be filled or covered with His glory and this is possible through the exercise of the knowledge of God, in kindness, justice, and righteousness. All human activities on earth must be targeted towards advancing these virtues and values, for this is the life that God delights in and this is the essence of life - living out these values!

For the earth to be filled with the knowledge of the glory of the Lord, we must take the kingdom into various spheres in our nation including the: Social, Government, Business, Education, Media, Entertainment and Sports. These are the seven mountains of influence or what we also call as the seven major spheres of life. Our work is to penetrate and invade these spheres of life using our gifts, talents and all we have.

Our calling lies in invading these terrains with the knowledge of God, His kindness, justice and righteousness, relating with men purposefully for kingdom influence and transformation. We are destined to bring about changes in our generation and fill the earth with knowledge of the glory of the Lord.

THIS IS THE TRUE ESSENCE AND VALUE OF LIFE!!!

GOLDEN NUGGET

1. It is time to sit up, put on your seat belt, fly high and soar to new dimensions.

2. God's intention is to transform your life, your promised land and your nation in order to use you in bringing back the earth to Himself.

3. The earnest attachment and profound devotion of your life should be to know the Lord and understand his kindness, justice, and righteousness in order to exercise these values in your journey of life.

4. Choose the real essence of life and pour your life into that which never fades – the kingdom of God.

5. What you see and keep thinking can affect what directions your life heads.

6. When you focus bears the eternal imprints of the kingdom, your essence for living would be singular.

7. There are seven spheres of life; Social, Government, Business, Education, Media, Entertainment and Sports. Our work is to penetrate and invade these spheres of life with all we have.

CONCLUSION

Friends, the life you have being given is the greatest gift of trust from God. It's to be lived ones. Remember, life on earth is just a dot in eternity. How you live your life on earth at the moment will determine how you will live eternity.

Since your life was given to you by God, then you ought to live it exactly the way he wants it lived. Life is like a borrowed textbook that will be returned to its owner after some times. You won't want to miss handle it because it's not yours. Do not miss handle life by living for selfish gains. Never live for wisdom, power and riches as you have learnt in the previous chapters. Live for God's glory now, live for kindness, justice and righteousness. Do not resist the purpose of God by saying no to kindness, justice and righteousness. Pharaoh did that when God wanted him to set his people free, and he ended in destruction.

These are according to God the true essence and values of life. God is interested in His glory and praise covering the earth, but only through the knowledge of God, only through His love and kindness, only by His justice and through His righteousness. All human activities on earth must be to advance and promote these core values. No life delights God better than a life that is dedicated to these values.

The best way to maximize and enjoy life is by making tangible changes and impact one day at a time. Do not procrastinate. There is nothing like a perfect timing. Do not say I will start living life after school or after my wedding, some may say they are waiting for their children to be matured before they start living out God's purpose. Remember, anyone that observes the wind will not sow and the one that observes the cloud will never reap. Why not start now, start from your backyard. Start with what you have. Make the best use of it.

Do not be like the man with the one talent Jesus talked about in the bible. His master gave him and two other fellow talents according to their abilities. The other folks multiplied their talents and had double of what they were given. But he hid his in the ground. Living a life that isn't impacting anyone is hearkened to you hiding your talent. Go out there and multiply your gifts. There are so many treasures in you. Bring out your best to your world. Do not wait. Put your foot prints on the sand of time This is action time, so, shake your world..

SINNER'S PRAYER OF SALVATION

Heavenly Father! I come to You in prayer, confessing all of my sins. I believe that You accept everyone who comes to You. Lord, forgive me of all my sins, have mercy on me.

I don't want to live this way anymore. I want to belong to You, Jesus! Come into my heart and cleanse me. Be my Saviour and my Lord. Guide me. I believe You died for my sins and was raised for my justification.

I confess You, Jesus Christ as my Lord. I thank You that You hear my prayer and I accept my salvation by faith. I thank You, my Saviour, for accepting me just as I am.

Amen.

If you sincerely prayed this prayer, God heard you and forgave you all your sins. Now, God is Your Father, and Jesus is Your Friend. Read the Bible, live with God and pray.

Thank you for reading this far. I really can't wait to hear what becomes of you through the application of these truths and principles. Feel free to write me at any time to my personal email- pastor@godembassy.org

You can also avail yourself of other training materials of mine available on my blog at www.SundayAdelajaBlog.com

For The Love of God, Church and Nation

SUNDAY ADELAJA'S
BIOGRAPHY

Pastor Sunday Adelaja is the Founder and Senior Pastor of The Embassy of the Blessed Kingdom of God for All Nations Church in Kyiv, Ukraine.

Sunday Adelaja is a Nigerian-born Leader, Thinker, Philosopher, Transformation Strategist, Pastor, Author and Innovator who lives in Kiev, Ukraine.

At 19, he won a scholarship to study in the former Soviet Union. He completed his master's program in Belorussia State University with distinction in journalism.

At 33, he had built the largest evangelical church in Europe — The Embassy of the Blessed Kingdom of God for All Nations.

Sunday Adelaja is one of the few individuals in our world who has been privileged to speak in the United Nations, Israeli Parliament, Japanese Parliament and the United States Senate.

The movement he pioneered has been instrumental in reshaping lives of people in the Ukraine, Russia and about 50 other nations where he has his branches.

His congregation, which consists of ninety-nine percent white Europeans, is a cross-cultural model of the church for the 21st century.

His life mission is to advance the Kingdom of God on earth by raising a generation of history makers who will live for a cause larger, bigger and greater than themselves. Those who will live like Jesus and transform every sphere of the society in every nation as a model of the Kingdom of God on earth.

His economic empowerment program has succeeded in raising over 200 millionaires in the short period of three years.

Sunday Adelaja is the author of over 300 books, many of which are translated into several languages including Russian, English, French, Chinese, German, etc.

His work has been widely reported by world media outlets such as The Washington Post, The Wall Street Journal, New York Times, Forbes, Associated Press, Reuters, CNN, BBC, German, Dutch and French national television stations.

Pastor Sunday is happily married to his "Princess" Bose Dere-Adelaja. They are blessed with three children: Perez, Zoe and Pearl.

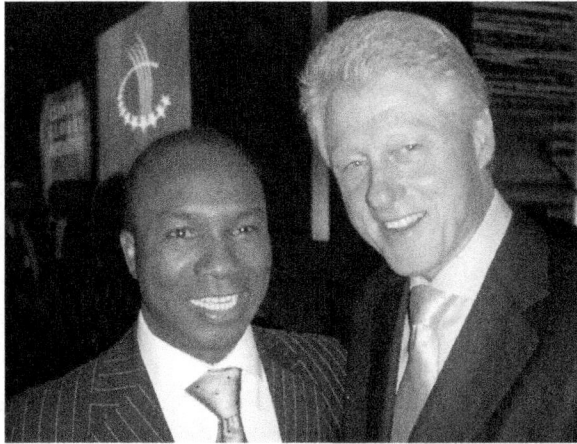

Bill Clinton —
42Nd President Of The
United States (1993–2001),
Former Arcansas State
Governor

Ariel "Arik" Sharon —
Israeli Politician, Israeli
Prime Minister (2001–2006)

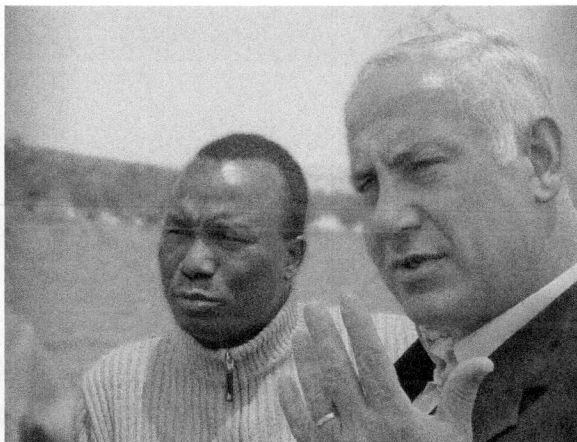

Benjamin Netanyahu —
Statesman Of Israel. Israeli
Prime Minister (1996–1999),
Acting Prime Minister
(From 2009)

Jean ChrEtien —
Canadian Politician,
20th Prime Minister Of
Canada, Minister Of Justice
Of Canada, Head Of Liberan
Party Of Canada

Rudolph Giuliani —
American Political Actor,
Mayor Of New York Served
From 1994 To 2001. Actor
Of Republican Party

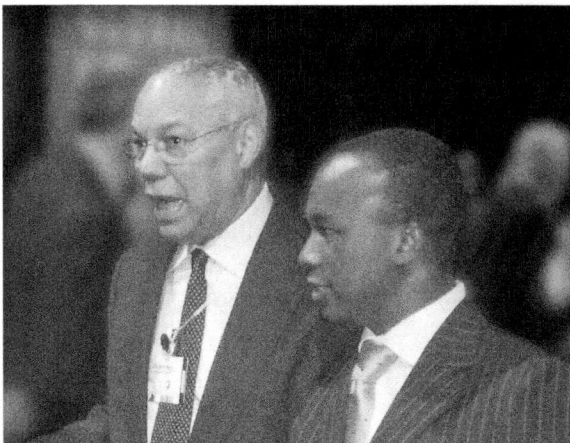

Colin Powell —
Is An American Statesman
And A Retired Four-Star
General In The Us Army,
65th United States Secretary
Of State

Peter J. Daniels —
Is A Well-Known And
Respected Australian
Christian International
Business Statesman Of
Substance

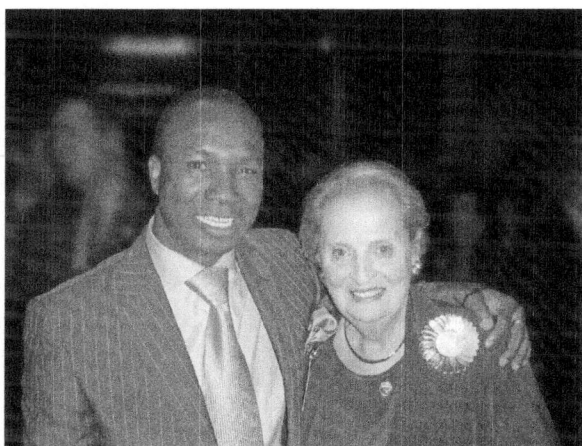

Madeleine
Korbel Albright —
An American Politician And
Diplomat, 64Th United States
Secretary Of State

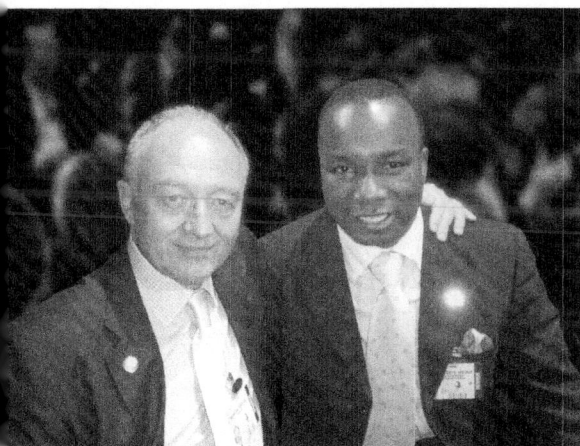

Kenneth Robert
Livingstone —
An English Politician,
1St Mayor Of London
(4 May 2000 – 4 May
2008), Labour Party
Representative

Sir Richard Charles Nicholas Branson — English Business Magnate, Investor And Philanthropist. He Founded The *Virgin Group*, Which Controls More Than 400 Companies

Mel Gibson — American Actor And Filmmaker

Chuck Norris — American Martial Artist, Actor, Film Producer And Screenwriter

Christopher Tucker — American Actor And Comedian

Bernice Albertine King — American Minister Best Known As The Youngest Child Of Civil Rights Leaders Martin Luther King Jr. And Coretta Scott King Andrew

Andrew Young — American Politician, Diplomat, And Activist, 14Th United States Ambassador To The United Nations, 55Th Mayor Of Atlanta

General Wesley
Kanne Clark —
4-Star General And Nato
Supreme Allied Commander

Dr. Sunday Adelaja's family:
Perez, Pearl, Zoe and Pastor Bose Adelaja

FOLLOW
SUNDAY ADELAJA
ON SOCIAL MEDIA

Subscribe And Read Pastor Sunday's Blog:
www.sundayadelajablog.com
Follow these links and listen to over 200
of Pastor Sunday's Messages free of charge:
http://sundayadelajablog.com/content/
Follow Pastor Sunday on Twitter:
www.twitter.com/official_pastor

Join Pastor Sunday's Facebook page to stay in touch:
www.facebook.com/pastor.
sunday.adelaja
Visit our websites for more
information about Pastor
Sunday's ministry:
http://www.godembassy.com
http://www.pastorsunday.com
http://sundayadelaja.de

CONTACT

FOR DISTRIBUTION OR TO ORDER
BULK COPIES OF THIS BOOK,
PLEASE CONTACT US:

USA

CORNERSTONE PUBLISHING

info@thecornerstonepublishers.com

+1 (516) 547-4999

www.thecornerstonepublishers.com

AFRICA

CHIOMA NWIGWE

E-mail: dsabooksplanet@gmail.com

+2347065228537, +2348122219291

UNITED KINDGOM

ADEKUNLE BANJOKO

Banjokoadekunle@gmail.com

+447411937793

KIEV, UKRAINE

pa@godembassy.org

Mobile: +380674401958

BEST SELLING BOOKS BY DR. SUNDAY ADELAJA
AVAILABLE ON AMAZON.COM AND OKADABOOKS.COM

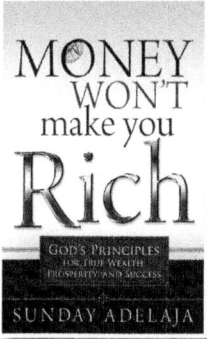

MONEY WON'T make you Rich
GOD'S PRINCIPLES FOR TRUE WEALTH PROSPERITY AND SUCCESS
SUNDAY ADELAJA

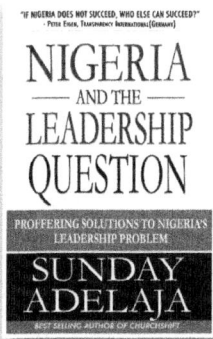

"IF NIGERIA DOES NOT SUCCEED, WHO ELSE CAN SUCCEED?"
- PETER EIGEN, TRANSPARENCY INTERNATIONAL (GERMANY)
NIGERIA AND THE LEADERSHIP QUESTION
PROFFERING SOLUTIONS TO NIGERIA'S LEADERSHIP PROBLEM
SUNDAY ADELAJA
BEST SELLING AUTHOR OF CHURCHSHIFT

MYLES MUNROE
... FINDING ANSWERS TO WHY GOOD PEOPLE DIE TRAGIC AND EARLY DEATHS
SUNDAY ADELAJA

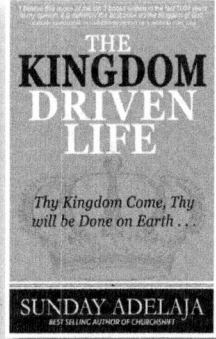

THE KINGDOM DRIVEN LIFE
Thy Kingdom Come, Thy will be Done on Earth . . .
SUNDAY ADELAJA
BEST SELLING AUTHOR OF CHURCHSHIFT

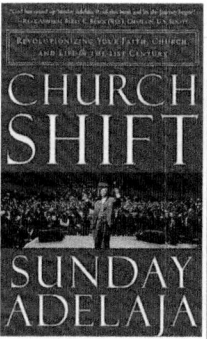

CHURCH SHIFT
SUNDAY ADELAJA

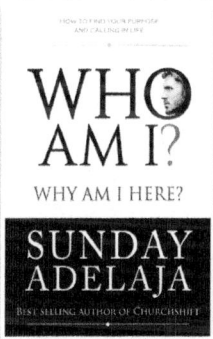

HOW TO FIND YOUR PURPOSE AND CALLING IN LIFE
WHO AM I? WHY AM I HERE?
SUNDAY ADELAJA
BEST SELLING AUTHOR OF CHURCHSHIFT

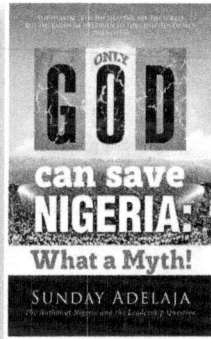

ONLY GOD can save NIGERIA: What a Myth!
SUNDAY ADELAJA
The Author of Nigeria and the Leadership Question

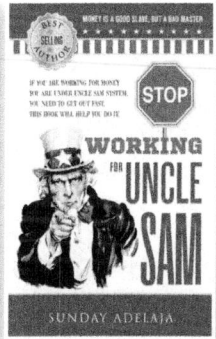

MONEY IS A GOOD SLAVE, BUT A BAD MASTER
BEST SELLING AUTHOR
IF YOU ARE WORKING FOR MONEY YOU ARE UNDER UNCLE SAM SYSTEM. YOU NEED TO GET OUT FAST. THIS BOOK WILL HELP YOU DO IT
STOP WORKING FOR UNCLE SAM
SUNDAY ADELAJA

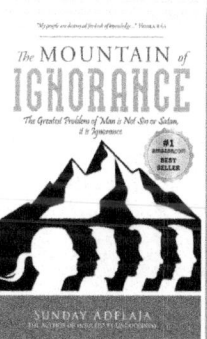

The MOUNTAIN of IGNORANCE
The Greatest Problem of Man is Not Sin or Satan, it is Ignorance
SUNDAY ADELAJA

OLORUNWA

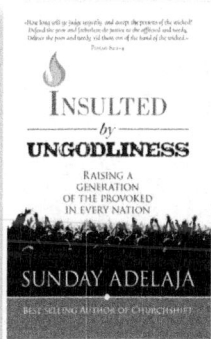

INSULTED by UNGODLINESS
RAISING A GENERATION OF THE PROVOKED IN EVERY NATION
SUNDAY ADELAJA
BEST SELLING AUTHOR OF CHURCHSHIFT

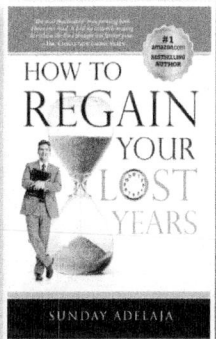

HOW TO REGAIN YOUR LOST YEARS
SUNDAY ADELAJA

BEST SELLING BOOKS BY DR. SUNDAY ADELAJA
AVAILABLE ON AMAZON.COM AND OKADABOOKS.COM

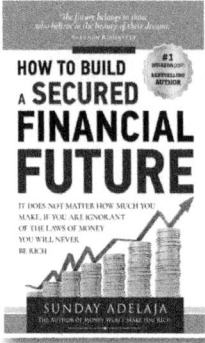

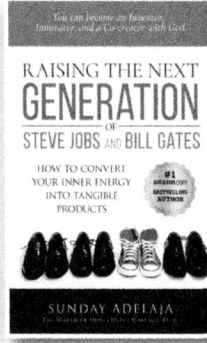

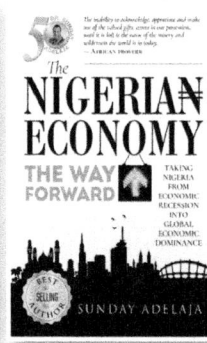

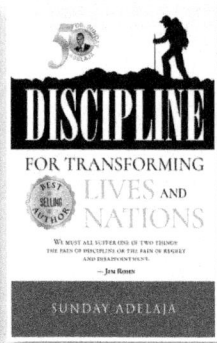

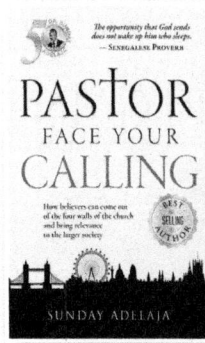

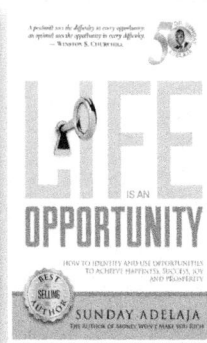

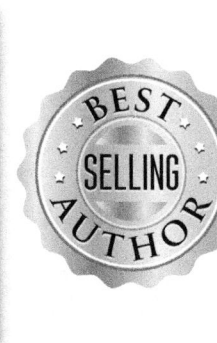

HOW TO BUILD A SECURED FINANCIAL FUTURE
SUNDAY ADELAJA

CREATE YOUR OWN NET WORTH
SUNDAY ADELAJA

RAISING THE NEXT GENERATION OF STEVE JOBS AND BILL GATES
HOW TO CONVERT YOUR INNER ENERGY INTO TANGIBLE PRODUCTS
SUNDAY ADELAJA

POVERTY MINDSET VS ABUNDANCE MINDSET
SUNDAY ADELAJA

WHY YOU MUST URGENTLY BECOME A WORKAHOLIC
SUNDAY ADELAJA

HOW TO BECOME GREAT THROUGH TIME CONVERSION
SUNDAY ADELAJA

The NIGERIAN ECONOMY THE WAY FORWARD
SUNDAY ADELAJA

DISCIPLINE FOR TRANSFORMING LIVES AND NATIONS
SUNDAY ADELAJA

PASTOR FACE YOUR CALLING
SUNDAY ADELAJA

WHERE THERE IS PROBLEM THERE IS MONEY
SUNDAY ADELAJA

LIFE IS AN OPPORTUNITY
SUNDAY ADELAJA

BEST SELLING AUTHOR

GOLDEN JUBILEE SERIES BOOKS
BY DR. SUNDAY ADELAJA

1. Who Am I
2. Only God Can Save Nigeria
3. The Mountain Of Ignorance
4. Stop Working For Uncle Sam
5. Poverty Mindset Vs Abundance Mindset
6. Raising The Next Generation Of Steve Jobs And Bill Gates
7. How To Build A Secured Financial Future
8. How To Become Great Through Time Conversion
9. Create Your Own Net Worth
10. Why You Must Urgently Become A Workaholic
11. How To Regain Your Lost Years
12. Pastor, Face Your Calling
13. Discipline For Transforming Lives And Nations
14. Excellence Your Key To Elevation
15. No One Is Better Than You
16. Problems Your Shortcut To Prominence
17. Let Heroes Arise!
18. How To Live An Effective Life
19. How To Win In Life
20. The Creative And Innovative Power Of A Genius
21. The Veritable Source Of Energy
22. The Nigerian Economy. The Way Forward
23. How To Get What You Need In Life
24. 7 Tips To Self-Fulfillment
25. Life Is An Opportunity
26. The Essence And Value Of Life
27. A Visionless Life Is A Meaningless Life
28. Where There Is Problem There Is Money
29. Work Is Better Than Vacation, Labour Better Than Favour
30. How To Overcome The Fear Of Death
31. Discovering The Purpose And Calling Of Nations
32. How To Become A Developed Nation Throught The Dignity Of Labor
33. Your Greatnes Is Proportional
34. Why Losing Your Job Is The Best Thing That Could Happen To You
35. What Do You Do With Your Time
36. Life Is Predictable
37. How To Be In The Here And Now
38. I Am A Person. Am I A Personality?
39. Discover The Source Of Your Latent Energy
40. How To Form Value Systems In A Child
41. Why I Am Unlucky
42. Hello! I Am Searching For Problems
43. Holistic Personality
44. How To transform And Build a Civilized Nation
45. Could You Be The Abraham Of Your Nation
46. The teambuilding skills of Jesus
47. How to keep your focus
48. The sin of irresponsibility
49. How Africans Brought Civilization To Europe
50. The Danger Of Monoculturalism

FOR DISTRIBUTION OR TO ORDER BULK COPIES OF THIS BOOKS, PLEASE CONTACT US:

USA | CORNERSTONE PUBLISHING
E-mail: info@thecornerstonepublishers.com, +1 (516) 547-4999
www.thecornerstonepublishers.com

AFRICA | CHIOMA NWIGWE
E-mail: dsabooksplanet@gmail.com
+2347065228537, +2348122219291

LONDON, UK | ADEKUNLE BANJOKO
E-mail: banjokoadekunle@gmail.com, +447411937793

KIEV, UKRAINE |
E-mail: pa@godembassy.org, Mobile: +380674401958

Printed in Great Britain
by Amazon